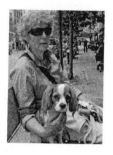

R. A. SCOTTI

Vanished Smile

R. A. Scotti is the author of three previous works
of nonfiction, including *Basilica: The Splendor
and the Scandal—Building St. Peter's* and *Sudden Sea: The Great Hurricane of 1938*, and four
novels. She lives in New York City.

www.rascotti.com

D0110779

"As full of twists, turns and suspense as any mystery novel. . . . Makes the Mona Lisa's story even more significant—and her smile even more alluring."
— *BookPage*

"Remarkable. . . . R. A. Scotti combines her skills as a historian and novelist to re-create this sensational crime, which has all the twists and turns of a mystery novel, except that it's true."
— *Florida Weekly*

"A book that nonfiction lovers, true-crime lovers, and especially art lovers will thoroughly enjoy."
— Curled Up With a Good Book

"Who needs *The Da Vinci Code* when you can have the real thing?"
— The Daily Beast

"An apt tribute to Leonardo da Vinci's mysterious muse. . . . In *Vanished Smile,* R. A. Scotti deftly uncovers the mysterious theft of the art world's prima donna. . . . Thanks to Scotti's meticulous research and atmospheric writing, a crime that had all the trappings of insanity, national prestige and obsession is brought to light marvelously."
— *The Business Standard*

"A crime caper . . . that conveys *l'air du temps.* . . . Enthralling."
— *Financial Times*

VANISHED SMILE

VANISHED SMILE

The Mysterious Theft of Mona Lisa

R. A. SCOTTI

VINTAGE BOOKS

A DIVISION OF RANDOM HOUSE, INC.

NEW YORK

Grateful acknowledgment is made to Anvil Press Poetry for
permission to reprint an excerpt from "The Little Car" from
Guillaume Apollinaire: Selected Poems, translated by Oliver Bernard
(London: Anvil Press Poetry, 2004). Reprinted by permission
of Anvil Press Poetry.

Grateful acknowledgment is made to Milton Esterow for permission to
use translations of French newspapers from his book, *The Art Stealers*.

The Library of Congress has cataloged the Knopf edition as follows:
Scotti, R. A.
Vanished smile : the mysterious theft of Mona Lisa / R. A. Scotti—1st ed.
p. cm.
1. Leonardo, da Vinci, 1452–1519. Mona Lisa.
2. Art thefts—France—Paris. I. Title.
ND623 L5A7 2009
759.5—dc22 2008047851

Vintage ISBN: 978-0-307-27838-8

Author photograph © Francesca E. M. Chigounis
Book design by M. Kristen Bearse

www.vintagebooks.com

For my mother and first reader
who slipped away from her own museum
August 16, 2007

The only thing that's important is the legend created by the picture, and not whether it continues to exist itself.

—PABLO PICASSO

CONTENTS

Map   x

A Perfect Crime   1

The Vanishing Act   7

The Hunt   27

The Blank Wall   63

Not the Usual Suspects   77

The Mystery Woman   119

A Letter from Leonardo   155

The Sting   189

A Perfect Story   209

The Prisoner   219

Acknowledgments   229

Notes   231

Bibliography   237

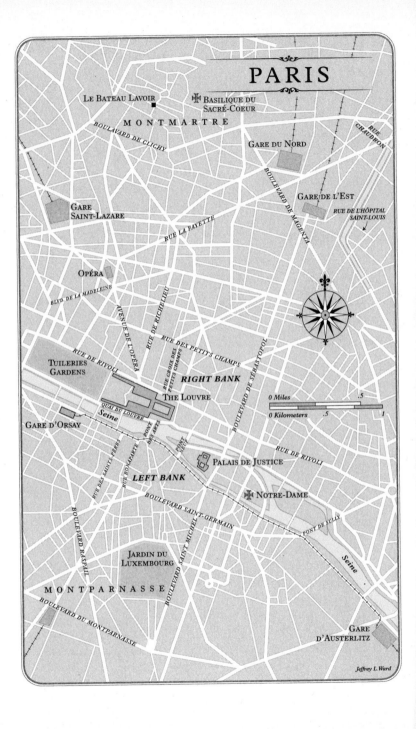

A PERFECT CRIME

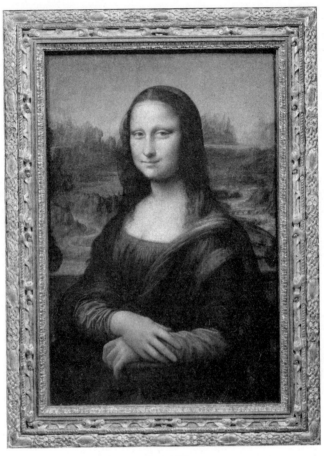

MONA LISA
(Courtesy of Erich Lessing/Art Resource, New York)

I

ACCORDING TO THE SONG, it's not supposed to rain when it's April in Paris, but the day was wet and raw. I dashed from my hotel room overlooking the Tuileries Gardens, across Rue de Rivoli, and took refuge in the Louvre. There were no ticket lines or tourist groups, and the vastness of the museum swallowed the few visitors, leaving the illusion that I had the whole place to myself. I skipped up the wide front stairs past the *Winged Victory,* imagining myself Audrey Hepburn in *Funny Face.*

The Louvre contains the history of France within its walls—courts, coups, royal weddings, revolution, hangings, and assassination. Henri IV bled to death from the knife of the assassin Ravaillac beneath the frescoed ceiling in the Galerie d'Apollon. The Louvre was a fortress in the Middle Ages, a palace in the monarchy, the people's museum in the Revolution, and Napoleon's showcase in the First Empire. It has stabled horses, sheltered squatters, and served as a printing house, an assignation spot for prostitutes, and studios for artists. David and Fragonard once lived and worked in the area below the Grande Galerie; family wash hung out on clotheslines, heated arguments and cooking flavors filtering up into the galleries. When Napoleon became emperor, he evicted the painters, complaining that one day they would burn down his museum.

I was wandering through the galleries without a guidebook

or floor plan when I came upon Mona Lisa, suddenly, unexpectedly, hanging in the center of one wall. The framed painting was enclosed in a glass box. It was sometime in the late 1970s and there was no special guard or protective rope forcing visitors to keep their distance. On the Louvre wall, she appeared dark, her colors muddy, her attitude aloof. Leonardo wrote that a painter should avoid positioning his subject in the full sun where the light and shadows are strong. She appears different to me now.

I have been living for months with Mona Lisa, teasing out the answer to a century-old mystery. In my narrow room, framed in a single long window, the shutters open to a slant of northern light, she has the colors of the Tuscan countryside. Her complexion is a soft golden shade. It doesn't matter that she has spent nearly her entire life in France or that the French call her *la Joconde* and claim her as a national treasure. Mona Lisa is as essentially Italian as Sophia Loren. Seductive yet serenely contained, instantly recognizable yet ever elusive.

In 2004 and 2005, an international team of specialists assembled at the Louvre to lift Mona Lisa's "veil of mystery." They analyzed Leonardo's artistry and science using the most sophisticated technology—radiography, 3-D scanners, microfluorescence, infrared reflectography, chemical and gas chromatography of the paint, and more. No work of art has ever undergone such intensive scrutiny. *Mona Lisa: Inside the Painting* presents their analyses, confirming in fascinating and exhaustive detail what the astute art patron Cassiano dal Pozzo wrote in 1625: Mona Lisa "lacks only the power of speech."

Her posture is perfect, her shoulders straight, hands folded one across the other. She wears no jewelry, not even a wedding ring. If she reached a hand out, the gesture would seem perfectly natural. Her face is wide at the cheekbones, the forehead high, the chin pointed. Her nose is narrow, her lips pale and closed, the corners turned up ever so slightly in the famous smile. More than the smile, though, it is the eyes that captivate. They are warm, brown, and inescapable.

Mona Lisa only has eyes for me. There is no other. No one more interesting, more intelligent, more compelling. And what is extraordinary, if a dozen others crowd into this room, each one will feel the same. Each person who looks at her becomes the only person in her world. It is flattering and, at the same time, maddening, because she gives away nothing of herself.

I close my eyes and imagine that she has vanished.

2

THE MYSTERY OF MONA LISA that I am pursuing begins in Paris at the end of the Belle Époque, when the city was poised at the cusp of an irreverent new century and an irreverent new art. In the brief *avant-guerre* interlude before trench warfare and unutterable loss, a burst of glorious incandescent energy made the City of Lights electric. Extraordinary young talents in many mediums from many nations trooped to Paris to perform their high-wire acts: the Russians Diaghilev and Stravinsky, the Italian Modigliani, the Spaniards Juan Gris and Pablo Picasso, and the man without a country Guillaume Apollinaire.

From the ateliers of Montmartre and the cafés of Montparnasse, a radical creative idiom was emerging that would change both art and writing. While Proust was wresting *The Remembrance of Things Past* from a pile of notes and scribbles, the very sentiment of remembrance was coming under attack. The past was no longer a lesson to be mastered. It was an inhibition to be overcome.

Paris then was as critical to the future of art as Florence was in the Renaissance, and the preeminent painter of each period—the celebrated master Leonardo da Vinci and the brash young contender Pablo Picasso—became central players in a crime so brazen and so brilliant that it would capture the attention of the world.

A century later, the mystery lingers, the truth as elusive as the prize. Who stole Mona Lisa?

THE VANISHING ACT

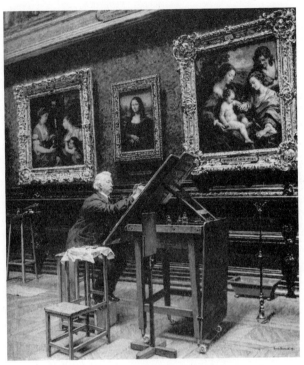

LOUIS BÉROUD PAINTING IN THE SALON CARRÉ
Painter Louis Béroud had been copying Mona Lisa.
When he returned to complete his painting on
Tuesday, August 22, 1911, he made a startling discovery.
(Courtesy of Réunion des Musées Nationaux/Art Resource, New York)

I

EARLY IN MAY, with the Hudson glassy beneath a morning haze, an elegant Latin American "marqués" stepped off the gangway of the S.S. *Mauritania*. He carried a Louis Vuitton case. The ship had been delayed for an extra day in quarantine at the mouth of the harbor awaiting clearance. At first light, the *Mauritania* was released, and like a dowager queen ignoring the minion tugs hauling and chugging, she began a stately glide up the river to a berth on the west bank of Manhattan island.

No magical skyline emerged through the lavender mist. The year was 1911, before the vertical city was invented. The steel and glass skyscrapers would come later, once Otis's new mechanical lift was accepted as something more than a risky contraption.

With a tip of his homburg to the ladies gathered on the first-class deck, the marqués slipped through the crowd, hastening without seeming to. Impatience makes fools of clever men, and he was careful never to convey the impression of a man in a hurry. In his work, patience and precision were paramount, and he had perfected both virtues, although he was not a virtuous man.

His passport, which had been issued in Argentina, identified him as Eduardo de Valfierno. Although he had used a dozen of the more common Spanish names, this was the alias that clung. The surname had been conferred by a caustic acquaintance. The title was his own addition. In his passport, every page was stamped with visas, indicating that he was both a man of the world and never long in a single place. The contents of his luggage indicated his occupation.

The marqués passed through New York customs, declaring that he had in his possession one Mona Lisa, and went directly downtown. The *Mauritania* was his sixth Atlantic crossing in a year, and on each trip, he had carried a Mona Lisa in his Vuitton luggage. He aroused no suspicion. New mechanical methods of printing were making reproductions ubiquitous, and increasingly, travelers were returning from the Grand Tour with copies of masterworks.

If the customs inspectors had been better versed in the traffic of art or the marqués less imposing in his demeanor and dress, he might not have sailed through with such ease, because the Mona Lisa he carried was a wood panel apparently of great age, not a painting on canvas.

From the rolled brim of his homburg to the tips of his gray doeskin gloves, the Marqués de Valfierno appeared to be a gentleman of means and refinement. An imperial bearing and courtly manners gave him a distinction that opened palace gates in Europe and made him an honored guest in the nouveau-riche mansions going up along Fifth Avenue. Envious colleagues groused that "his front was worth a million dollars."

By the time the marqués reached the financial district, a commotion of horse-drawn hansom cabs, milk wagons, peddlers' carts, motorized cars from the R. E. Olds Company in Detroit, new Model T Fords, and the first "autostages" with seats for a dozen riders clogged the cobblestone streets. Carrying the Vuitton case, the marqués entered the stony sanctuary of a downtown bank. The space was as cavernous as a basilica, the atmosphere hushed. Vaulted ceilings and marble floors bespoke an architecture chosen to inspire faith that capital would be closely guarded and investors' secrets held fast.

In the privacy of a windowless room in a safe-deposit vault, he opened the case, removed the painting, and with extreme care, placed it beside five others. Each was a flawless fake—an exact and brilliant forgery.

That evening the Marqués de Valfierno—in translation, "the Marquis of the Gate of Hell"—would dress in white tie and tails and linger over brandy in a private dining room set with white damask, crystal candelabra, and vases of calla lilies. His dinner companion would be a man of substance. Clouded in curls of cigar smoke and eased by the finest wines and champagne, the marqués would make his irresistible pitch.

The scheme itself was a work of art. He would offer, for a kingly price, the most coveted woman in the world. He would confide that his was a rare offer, extended only to the six wealthiest, most discerning men, each a renowned collector of priceless art and beautiful objects. The offer would never be repeated. Whichever man placed the highest bid would win. Although, as a point of honor, he could not be more specific, in the course of the conversation, certain names were mentioned—Morgan, Mellon, Carnegie, Huntington, Altman.

In the eighteenth century, the English were the "barbarians [who were] buying up everything."* Now it was the Americans' turn. Freshly minted millionaires were sweeping across Europe, amassing art with the same lack of scruples that they had amassed fortunes, forming many of the great collections (Frick, Morgan, Carnegie, Mellon, Widener, and Huntington, whose wife described him as "scrupulously dishonest"). For

* 1760, Johann Winckelmann.

continental conmen like the marqués, separating American magnates from their millions had become an art form and lucrative profession. Sharks at home, the Americans were innocents abroad—irresistible targets for every kind of scam. None was more clever or daring than the Mona Lisa caper.

1911 was a year of grand escapades. In the boatyards of Belfast, a magnificent new ocean liner was under construction. Its builders boasted that it would be "unsinkable." In Antarctica, Captain Robert Falcon Scott was trudging across the frozen plateau to the South Pole, the Union Jack folded in his pack, dreaming of making history, and in Paris, a plan was brewing to pinch the most famous painting in the world. Of these three grand escapades, the first seemed assured of success, the second likely, and the third not only improbable but impossible.

2

SUNDAY IN THE LOUVRE WITH LISA. Another scorching day in Paris, ninety-five degrees Fahrenheit, no hint of a breeze, no hope of a shower. The air was close, the sun so blazing that even the carriage horses were wearing straw hats. For more than fifty days, temperatures had rarely dropped below ninety degrees. The country beyond Paris was burning. Thatch-roofed farmhouses and acres of parched forest had become tinder, and spontaneous-combustion fires broke out near Poitiers, Orléans, and Beaumont, Albertville, Dijon, and Fontainebleau.

Within the galleries of the Louvre Museum, even in the late afternoon of August 20, the heat was a physical presence so overwhelming that it trivialized four thousand years of art and history. Maximilien Alphonse Paupardin slumped on his stool in the doorway of the Salon Carré, as sated and overstuffed as a Rembrandt burgher. He was weighed down by the weather and by an unseasonable midday meal. In everything except name, Paupardin was a simple man who felt elevated in a uniform—first in an army uniform and now in the costume of a Louvre guard. A uniform gave him stature, confidence, a defined place in the world. Out of uniform, he felt diminished.

He was ignorant of the history that surrounded him. He knew nothing of the medieval knights in suits of mail who had staved off Anglo-Norman invaders from the parapets of Fortress Louvre or the lusty young kings, François I and Louis XIV, a Valois and a Bourbon respectively, who, imagining Paris as a new Rome, had turned the Louvre fortress into a palace fit for a Caesar. Paupardin knew only one emperor, the cocky little Corsican and epic pillager, Napoleon Bonaparte.

On an average day, several hundred visitors would traipse through the galleries—students, artists, foreign travelers, and Frenchmen from the provinces—but visitors were few on this Sunday afternoon at the end of summer. An occasional tourist had wandered through from the Grande Galerie, not staying long enough to arouse the guard's interest or register in his memory. He stirred on his stool, his nap arrested.

Had a ripple of gas disturbed him, his midday meal returning? Did he catch a sudden whiff of oleander or hear an alien sound? He raised an eyelid. Three "macaroni" were whispering together. The old guard glanced at them with disdain. They were dressed in their Sunday best, black suits and straw boaters, but no suit could disguise what they were—young working-class men who had immigrated to Paris from the mountain towns of northern Italy looking for work and, more often than not, finding trouble.

There was one other visitor. The boy had returned with

flowers. A young Goethe enamored of all things Italian. The guard recognized him, a quintessential German, hair flaxen, eyes ice blue, warmed now by the lust to possess the dark lady. He mooned over her, gazing into her liquid eyes, and she seemed to answer. Eyes are the mirror of the soul, her creator, Leonardo da Vinci, believed.

Men had been coming to court her for years, bearing flowers, notes, and poems that Paupardin scooped up and tossed out at the end of the day. She accepted their attentions democratically but gave nothing in return, just the same half-smile. She conferred it on all equally. A promise, a tease, a warning. No man could be sure. The lovesick boy would return the next day and the day after.

Like rival lovers paying suit, the three olive-skinned men watched the German. Bemused? Mocking? Wary? Their faces gleamed as if in rapture, features shining and dissolving in a heat so oppressive that, if *The Victory of Samothrace* were sculpted of wax, it would dissolve like the wings of Icarus. The flowers the boy proffered were already wilting.

Paupardin saw the visitors without seeing them, as he saw the paintings without seeing them, the masterpieces of the Louvre collection, each in its place, unchanged for decades. He was anticipating the next day, Monday, his day of rest, when the museum was closed for cleaning and the staff reduced.

The old guard pulled a soiled handkerchief from his pocket to mop his face, and caught her watching him. She was smiling as if she knew he had overindulged at noon and dozed on the job. It was the disconcerting smile of a mother or a mistress. He wiped his face to blot her out and sighed with resignation.

There were no youngsters among the custodians who guarded the patrimony of France. Age and lethargy were job requirements. Only retired noncommissioned officers of the French army could apply to be guards at the Musée du

Louvre. The country they had served allowed them one final tour of duty before relegating them to permanent pasture and probable penury. This was their last shuffle, and ambitions rarely if ever strayed beyond a good meal, an afternoon nap, or perhaps a few moments with a grandchild.

The guard shifted his substantial weight on the insubstantial stool and repressed a belch, regretting his choice of cassoulet, a dinner suitable for a winter Sunday, not the doldrums of August. The afternoon meandered in half-time. By four o'clock, when the bell clanged signaling the museum's closing, the "macaroni" and the young Goethe had disappeared.

Paupardin picked up the oleander and folded his stool. The Grande and Petite Galeries emptied, footsteps echoing, the many doors banging shut. Outside the Louvre, Paris shimmered in the glaze of heat. In the Tuileries Gardens just beyond, a halfhearted game of boule was ending.

Summer is not a popular season in Paris. Average August temperatures chase rich and poor to the vineyards of the Loire valley and the cooling beaches of Normandy. This August was the worst that Parisians forced by one circumstance or another to remain in town could remember in a dozen years. The heat wave had hung on for weeks. Less than one millimeter of rain had fallen in Paris during the entire month, and in a single day, four people had collapsed with sunstroke. At six o'clock, it was still ninety-one degrees. The cafés of Pigalle were deserted. The Seine stood still. Along its banks, the sheltering plane trees and chestnut trees drooped.

Night like liquid velvet settled over the mansard roofs, innocent, if a night is ever innocent. As Sunday merged with Monday and the city awakened to a new day, the game that would stun Paris and astound the world was afoot.

No one would notice for more than twenty-four hours.

3

THE FIRST GULP OF Tuesday, August 22, was as unsurprising as a glass of *vin ordinaire*. Water carts washed the cobbled streets. Workers in blue overalls swept the quais with faggot brooms. Under the girders and skylights at Les Halles, what Émile Zola called the belly of Paris, horses and workers performed the morning ballet, mongers shouting their products and prices through the central market. The bells of nearby St-Eustache tolled.

Louis Béroud followed the narrow Seine channel along Quai Saint-Michel. At the point where the Boulevard Saint-Michel disgorged, he crossed and continued along the Quai des Grands Augustins, perhaps stopping to look at the steeple of Sainte-Chapelle rising out of the cluster of government buildings that comprise the judicial heart of Paris, housing courtrooms, jail cells, and the office of the chief of the Paris police. Béroud may have stood once in the upper chapel, with sunlight fiery through the finest glass in Paris, and thought of God. The river was languid, the water level so low that the color had concentrated to a murky ocher. He decided not to cross at Pont Neuf, still called the "new bridge" though now it was the oldest in Paris, and he continued on to the Pont des Arts.

Paris saunters through history in the present tense, neither extolling its past nor rushing to embrace its future. If the analogy were extended to other capitals, Athens would exist in the past perfect, Rome in the past imperfect, New York in the future imperative. Perhaps because Paris was never the seat of empire, never the center of the world like Athens and Rome, its past is not preserved as a glorious ruin but incorporated into the present. At the same time, a bedrock conservatism prevents the avant-garde from being quickly accepted and instantly absorbed. New York, where nothing remains new for long, is a work in progress, a process as much as a place. There the new is seized and swallowed whole. But Paris responds to change with the caginess of a concierge, acutely curious yet deeply suspicious.

Louis Béroud belonged to a formal world that was passing with the Belle Époque. He was a fine-looking man in his mid-fifties, with strong, regular features and an abundance of white wavy hair. Béroud dressed conservatively in a black frock coat and striped trousers. His ideas were as traditional as his dress.

In the first decade of the twentieth century, there were as many "isms" in painting as there were in politics. Impressionism, as shocking as a glimpse of stocking not so long ago, now appeared tame enough for the parlor wall, and one artistic "ism" eclipsed the next in a dizzying rush to modernity—fauvism, symbolism, primitivism, and now cubism. (Surrealism and Dadaism would come later, like exclamation points after the folly of a war to end all war.)

To Béroud, the new painting by whatever name was a calculated attempt to destroy five centuries of art. He had earned a respectable following with a series of paintings using the various museum galleries as backgrounds, and he knew its labyrinth of rooms and galleries better than many of the curators and custodians.

The Louvre encouraged amateur painters, allowing them to copy the masters and store their easels and paint boxes overnight in the numerous nooks and closets recessed in the wall paneling. There was one stipulation: No canvas could be the same size as the original. It was a modest and mostly ineffectual effort to prevent forgery, which was endemic throughout Europe. Collecting had become a favorite sport of American tycoons, and the market for authentic art and artful frauds was reaching extraordinary heights.

This morning, Béroud intended to use his brush like an épée to vent his displeasure at a new museum policy. In an effort to adapt to modern times, the Louvre was introducing a number of innovations, and Béroud belonged to a vocal group that opposed them. One egregiously offensive "improvement" was the decision to place the most valuable paintings in three-dimensional protective frames. The first to suffer the indignity was Mona Lisa.

An Ingres had been slashed a few years before, and the director of national museums, Jean Théophile Homolle, had ordered the glass frames to shield the art from vandals and visitors. His motive may have been laudable, but a purist like Béroud was appalled. The glass box desecrated the communion of art and art lover. The glass was an intrusion that altered the light, created an unnatural reflection, and distorted the aesthetic experience.

Béroud arrived at the museum that August morning to register his displeasure. His idea was to paint a scene of a man shaving in the new glass that protected Mona Lisa, or perhaps a young girl using the glass as a mirror to do her hair.* Walking up the main staircase, he crossed into the Grande Galerie, exchanging pleasantries with the guards. Beneath a coffered ceiling, the broad hall extends more than twelve hundred feet, the length of four football fields. A stroll from end to end was both a gambol through the history of art and a walking tour of Europe from Holland to Italy.

At the Italian end of the gallery, Béroud turned into the Salon Carré, a gracious square gallery with a rare collection of paintings and a romantic history. Here, smiled on by the painted lady he called variously Madame Lisa and the Sphinx of the Occident, Napoleon had married Marie-Thérèse of

* Roy McMullen suggests the latter in his book Mona Lisa: *The Picture and the Myth.*

Austria to secure an heir and an alliance. After the ceremony, he crossed the gardens to the Tuileries Palace and settled the two women in his bedroom—his new bride and his Madame Lisa.

The Louvre owned the richest collection of sixteenth-century masterworks outside of Italy, and many of them were displayed in the Salon Carré—Titian's *Entombment of Christ,* Rembrandt's *Supper at Emmaus,* Correggio's *Betrothal of St. Catherine of Alexandria,* Raphael's *Holy Family,* Veronese's panoramic fresco *The Wedding Feast at Cana,* and Leonardo da Vinci's *la Joconde.*

On this Tuesday morning, her place on the wall was empty. All that remained were four iron hooks and a rectangular shape several shades deeper than the surrounding area—a ghostly image marking the space that Mona Lisa had filled. Except for a brief sojourn in Brest, where she was sent for safe-keeping during the Franco-Prussian War, she had hung in the Louvre since Napoleon was exiled to St. Helena.

Béroud was disappointed to find her absent. Setting down his easel and paint box, he called to the guard:

Brigadier Paupardin, where is Mona Lisa?

Being photographed, I suppose.

Paupardin displayed no concern. The institution of a photo-graphic studio in the Louvre was another innovation of Direc-tor Homolle, and a project to photograph the entire collection was under way. Paintings were regularly taken off to be copied. In case of damage, loss, or future restoration, the museum would have an accurate record of the original work.

The camera was becoming an indispensable instrument in the creation, conservation, and reproduction of art, and Director Homolle was so enthusiastic about the new medium that he allowed the photographers unlimited access. Any con-tract photographer or curator could saunter into a gallery and remove a painting from the wall without making a formal request, obtaining permission, or informing the guard. Because the paintings were simply hung on hooks—not even the most priceless masterpieces were wired or bolted—anyone could take them down and carry them off.

Béroud responded to Paupardin with a raised eyebrow and a shrug. So many changes and so few to his liking. Still, he accepted the inevitable with good humor.

Of course, Paupardin, when women are not with their lovers, they are apt to be with their photographers.

Depositing his easel and paints, Béroud left the museum. When he returned around eleven o'clock, the wall was still bare. Annoyed that his day was being wasted, he confronted the guard again.

Brigadier Paupardin, how long does a woman need to have her picture taken? The day is wasted. Do me a favor. Find out when she will return.

The guard sauntered off, pleased to have an excuse to leave his post and sneak an extra Gauloise. Since he was in no hurry to accomplish his mission, probably fifteen or so minutes elapsed before he eventually reached the studio and asked when Mona Lisa would be returning to the gallery. The photographers answered his question with stares as vacant as the Salon Carré wall. Mona Lisa was not sitting for her portrait.

Paupardin repeated his question more forcefully, as if it had been ignored the first time.

Mona Lisa, la Joconde . . . ?

No. We just told you. She is not here. No one has touched her.

The photographers suggested that he check other rooms: The painting might have been moved to a different gallery. Paupardin brushed them off. The Louvre collection was not a deck of cards, constantly being shuffled, and Mona Lisa was its prized possession. In all his years of employment, she had occupied the same wall space.

His eyes flicked across the studio quickly, then again, slowly scanning the room. His immediate reaction was confusion. Paintings don't step down off museum walls and walk away. Mona Lisa had been hanging in her usual place when he left on Sunday. On Monday, the museum was closed, and yet she was gone—lost or stolen or strayed. How do you mislay Mona Lisa, and worse, how do you explain it? The lethargy that was Paupardin's habitual demeanor lifted. Fear, like a swallow of vinegar, choked him. Leonardo da Vinci's most famous work, worth many more francs than Paupardin could earn if he had several lives, was missing on his watch.

He felt a lightness in his head. The mix of fear and confusion produces incoherence even in the sharpest minds, and Paupardin's mind was rusty at best. If he had lived a century or so earlier, he would not have been enshrined in the pantheon of Enlightenment philosophers. The old guard tore through the halls, running, lumbering, winded, shouting silently a single word: *MERDE!* Bursting into the director's office, Paupardin gasped out the stunning news:

La Joconde, c'est partie!

Director Homolle was vacationing in Mexico, and acting in his place was the curator of Egyptian antiquities, Georges Bénédite. To Paupardin, now verging on hysteria, the curator's response seemed excruciatingly slow in coming. Bénédite surveyed the flustered old guard with something between vexation and pity.

Mais oui, Monsieur le Custodien . . . A long pause separated each word. *La Joconde, c'est partie!*

The curator repeated the guard's absurdist message—Mona Lisa has left—as if to say the Eiffel Tower has fallen.

Mona Lisa had provoked false alarms and public pranks before. Just the previous year, in July 1910, a popular gossip sheet called *Le Cri de Paris* reported her missing and continued the hoax for weeks, claiming that she had been replaced with a copy. If she was not in her usual place, Bénédite had little doubt that she was not far off. He called in the supervisor of the museum guards, and the three men set off on a search through the picture galleries.

The skeptical curator visited the Salon Carré, examined the photo studios, and quizzed the staff. More than three hours had passed since Louis Béroud found her missing. If Paupardin was not crazed and the impossible had happened, precious time had been lost. Because phone lines were not secure, Bénédite went in person to the Palais de Justice and informed the chief of the Paris police.

4

AT ONE O'CLOCK, Louis Lépine, prefect of the Seine, arrived at the museum with an army of gendarmes. Every exit closed behind him. No one was allowed to enter or exit. A cordon of police encircled the building and took positions on the roof to intercept anyone attempting to skulk away. An additional sixty officers fanned out through the galleries, searching for the missing painting. Excuses were made to keep the public calm. The custodial staff was told that a water main had broken. Patience was urged. But a whisper was passing through the galleries and offices.

Prefect Lépine was a compact man whose habitual uniform was an old-fashioned morning coat and bowler hat. His size and stature were Napoleonic. His appearance and approach were Freudian. Lépine looked enough like Sigmund Freud to be his identical twin—same thinning white hair, same spectacles, same neatly pointed beard. As the chief of police in Paris, he was a political power, appointed by and accountable only to the

president of France. Lépine was not only the top law enforce-
ment officer in the nation's capital, he also controlled the fire
department and the transportation systems, and he could call
up the armed forces garrisoned in Paris in an emergency.

He wielded his considerable clout autocratically, which
earned him a number of nicknames—the "Pooh Bah of Paris,"
the "demi-mayor," "*le petit roi*," and "the little man with the
big stick." The "big stick" referred to the club that his police
were ordered to wield freely to maintain order. Lépine brought
elements of both Napoleon and Freud to his work. While he
was not squeamish about breaking heads, he also introduced
psychological methods of crowd control that attracted attention far beyond France.

While his men swept the galleries, he reviewed the facts
with Bénédite. It was not an official interrogation—that would
come later. First Lépine wanted to establish a sequence of
events. Unless Mona Lisa were found within the next few
hours, her disappearance would become a national scandal.
The government would have to be alerted—the vacationing
museum director, the chief of the national police, the minister
of the interior, the minister of fine arts, all the way up to the
president of the republic.

Curator Bénédite had only nine more days as acting director
before Homolle returned from vacation, and he wanted them
to pass peacefully. Bénédite believed there must be a simple
explanation, and he was anxious to keep the incident quiet
as long as possible. The facts, as he knew them, were scant.
Mona Lisa had been unaccounted for since early morning. Her
absence was first noted at nine o'clock, but she could have
been missing much longer. No one could vouch for her whereabouts on Monday—twenty-four hours as blank as the wall
where she had hung. The thieves—if there were thieves—
could be in Belgium, the Black Forest, the Riviera. They could
be on the high seas sailing for Buenos Aires or New York.

Lépine acted swiftly. By order of the prefect of the Seine, the Louvre was closed until further notice, and the borders of France were sealed. Nothing and no one would be allowed in or out without a thorough search. Trains and cars were stopped. Within hours, an international dragnet reached across three continents. Ships arriving and departing from any port in France since Sunday, August 20, would be detained when they reached their next port of call.

A curious crowd gathered on Rue de Rivoli, wondering why no one was allowed to enter the Louvre. Gendarmes blocked every door, giving nothing away. Inside, the police made their first discovery. Two frames were pushed into a corner of a service stairway a few yards from the Salon Carré. One was a three-dimensional glass box, obviously of recent construction. The other, which appeared to be of great value, was of antique carved wood and bore the label:

> LEONARDO DA VINCI (1452–1519)
> *École Florentine*
> LA JOCONDE
> (Portrait de Mona Lisa)

Bénédite identified it as a gift given just a few years before by the Countess de Béarn to frame the Leonardo. Both were intact, the wood undamaged, the glass unbroken. By all appearances, Mona Lisa had stepped out of her frames as effortlessly as a woman stepped out of her petticoats.

5

ON A MUNDANE MORNING in late summer in the heart of Paris, the impossible had happened. Mona Lisa had vanished.

On Sunday evening, August 20, 1911, Leonardo da Vinci's best-known painting, conservatively estimated at five million dollars ($112.5 million today), was hanging in her usual place on the wall of the Salon Carré, between Correggio's *Mystical Marriage* and Titian's *Allegory of Alfonso d'Avalos.* On Tuesday morning, when the Louvre reopened to the public, she was gone.

Within hours after the discovery of her empty frames, the story broke in an extra edition of *Le Temps,* the major morning newspaper in France. Along the grand boulevards of Paris, newsboys echoed Paupardin's cry: "*Mona Lisa, c'est partie!*"

Incredulous reporters from local papers and international news services converged on the museum. Paris was the hub for news from Europe, Africa, and the Near East, and there was a considerable press contingent. In addition to the numerous local papers, the city had four major news services—Agence Havas, Reuters, the Wolff Agency, and the Associated Press—as well as a number of foreign bureaus. *The New York Times* had opened a Paris office three years before, and its correspondent, Henri de Blowitz, arrived at the scene at about five-thirty p.m. Many perplexed Americans were still milling outside the gates, and Bénédite and his curators were speculating freely to the press.

"*La Joconde* is gone. That is all I can say," Bénédite told the *Times'* man. "So far we have not the slightest clue as to the perpetrator of the crime. How he or they came or left the premises is as yet a mystery. Why the theft was committed is also a mystery to me, as I consider the picture valueless in the hands of a private individual."

Paul Leprieur, the curator of paintings and drawings, went further. He was certain the painting had been stolen by someone who intended to return a good copy later, and he warned the thieves not to attempt such a fraud: "I have studied the picture for years, mounted and unmounted, know every minor detail of it, and would recognize a copy, however perfect, after five minutes' observation."

Prefect Lépine was clearly annoyed by the curators' loose talk. His men had found the frames, and he was confident they would soon find the painting. Until then he wanted to keep the public and the politicians calm. "The thieves—I am inclined to think there is more than one—got away with it, all right," he told the press. While conceding that there were a number of plausible motives, he said, "the more serious possibility is that *la Joconde* was stolen to blackmail the government."

If Mona Lisa were being held for ransom, Lépine expected a demand would be made within forty-eight hours.

THE HUNT

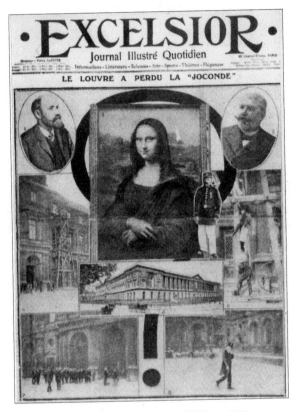

EXCELSIOR NEWSPAPER, AUGUST 23, 1911

On August 23, 1911, Mona Lisa's disappearance was a front-page story
in every Paris newspaper. Under the headline, LE LOUVRE A PERDU LA
"JOCONDE" (The Louvre Has Lost Mona Lisa), the illustrated paper
Excelsior published a photomontage. Surrounding Mona Lisa and
the Louvre are (top to bottom, left to right) the museum director
Jean Théophile Homolle, and the Sûreté chief Octave Hamard; two
views of a scaffold on the side of the Louvre, considered a possible
escape route for the thieves; police converging on the museum;
and Prefect Louis Lépine inside.

I

Wednesday, August 23

FOR ONCE, THE FAMOUSLY BLASÉ Parisians were non-plussed. Who could believe that a thief could lift Mona Lisa off the wall and waltz unnoticed out of the Louvre with the celebrated lady in his arms? Front-page stories in the Paris dailies echoed their shock. "The disappearance of *la Joconde* by Leonardo da Vinci surpasses the imagination," *Le Figaro* wrote.

"For many, the Mona Lisa is the Louvre," the *Paris-Journal* echoed. "In the eyes of the public, even the uneducated, the Mona Lisa occupies a privileged position that is not to be accounted for by its value alone."

The story traveled around the world as swiftly as telegraph and cable could carry it. On front pages in every major city, the dateline was Paris.

"The entire world sat back aghast," *The New York Times* reported. "Nothing like the theft of the Mona Lisa had ever been perpetrated before in the world's history."

In Milan, the *Corriere della Sera* ran an illustration of two thieves removing Mona Lisa with the headline:

COME SIA STATO POSSIBILE L'IMPOSSIBILE
HOW THE IMPOSSIBLE BECAME POSSIBLE

Rome wondered:

DOVE VA *LA GIOCONDA* DI LEONARDO?*
WHERE HAS *MONA LISA* GONE?

The London *Times* reported in thoroughly British under-
statement:

WHAT IS PERHAPS THE MOST FAMOUS
PICTURE IN THE LOUVRE
HAS BEEN SELECTED FOR ABSTRACTION

2

Mona Lisa had been spirited away, leaving no forwarding
address. Prefect Lépine called in the one person he believed
could illuminate her mystifying vanishing act. Alphonse
Bertillon, chief of the Department of Judicial Identity of the
Paris Prefecture, was the closest thing France had to the inter-
nationally popular Baker Street Regular, and Bertillon had the
advantage of being real.

Immaculate in dress and imperious in manner, Alphonse
Bertillon seemed as out of place at most crime scenes as the
Virgin Mary at the Folies-Bergère, but he was in his element at
the Louvre. He arrived with a magnifying glass, dusting powder, and a trail of assistants carrying bulky cameras and pre-
cisely constructed wooden boxes that held ink bottles and glass
plates, the tools of his trade. Waving aside the gendarmes
blocking entry to the museum, he proceeded directly to the
stairwell where the frames had been found. Bits of discolored

---

* Mona Lisa is called *la Gioconda* in Italian as well as *la Joconde* in French.

paper, remnants of the packing that had been stuffed between the frame and the painting to secure it, littered the floor.

With a white linen handkerchief in one hand and a magnifying glass in the other, Bertillon approached the empty frames as cautiously as a lion trainer who understands the imperfect line between the tame and the feral. The handkerchief prevented his own prints from compromising his investigation. The magnifying glass allowed him to examine each frame centimeter by centimeter.

Bertillon had introduced a revolutionary form of criminal examination called forensic detection. His father had been a pioneering anthropologist, and from his earliest years, Bertillon had displayed a keen interest in social adaptation. He believed that each person has a unique physiological profile. Using the color of the eyes, hair, and skin, and eleven bodily measurements, he devised a system to identify criminals. To complete the portrait, he photographed each suspect in full face and in profile, creating the first mug shots. Photography was an innovation in crime work. There was no infrared or ultraviolet photography then, and Bertillon experimented with color-sensitive plates and blinding ribbons of magnesium to illuminate crime scenes.

The Bertillon System of anthropometry appealed more to artists than to his colleagues. One of those intrigued was the young Spaniard Pablo Picasso, who was disrupting art circles in Paris with his cubist canvases. For local police departments, taking intricate skeletal measurements was laborious work, and around the same time that Bertillon was developing his criminal profile, a Scottish surgeon named Henry Faulds was trying to convince Scotland Yard that the whorls on the tips of the fingers were unique to each person. Fingerprinting proved a much handier tool for police, and it quickly overshadowed the Bertillon System.

Although he only grudgingly accepted fingerprinting as a

vital detection aid, Bertillon became a master at lifting prints. He was the first detective to win a murder conviction on the evidence of fingerprints alone, and his talent for detection became legendary. In *The Hound of the Baskervilles,* Sherlock Holmes is described as the "second highest expert in Europe," after the French savant.

Bertillon approached a crime scene like a surgeon preparing to operate. In the minutiae that others overlooked, he often found a revealing clue. Crowded into the narrow Louvre stairwell, he conducted a slow, meticulous examination of Mona Lisa's empty frames. Halfway up the glass on the left side of the box frame, he found a smudge. From a custom-built case containing instruments of varying sizes, compositions, and thicknesses, Bertillon selected a soft camel-hair brush. Dusting the frame with finely ground graphite, he lifted a perfect thumbprint. The Mona Lisa thief had left his calling card.

3

THE HUNT WAS ON. Political powers, museum administrators, and police brass rushed back to Paris from their August vacations and converged on the museum.

Behind the locked doors of the Louvre, a judicial inquest convened to interrogate witnesses, hear evidence, and issue arrest warrants. The presiding judge was Magistrate Henri Drioux, a solid cube of a man with a bald head, a pince-nez on a black cord, and a reputation for intimidating witnesses.

At the same time, Minister of Beaux Arts Théodore Steeg and his deputy, Henri Étienne Dujardin-Beaumetz, opened an administrative inquiry to explore how such a shocking incident could happen in the most august museum in France. Dujardin, an injudicious man, blustered that delinquent guards, conservators, or other responsible officials would receive no mercy.

Museum curators, led by Paul Leprieur, began compiling a dossier on Mona Lisa. Like a missing-persons report, the file contained the most recent series of photographs and a detailed description of her appearance, condition, and history. If and when she returned, the information could be compared with the recovered painting to determine authenticity.

In the Salon Carré, Prefect Lépine ordered Mona Lisa stolen again. Like a leading lady's understudy, another painting was fitted into her frames, and the theft was reenacted twice. The first time, gendarmes committed the crime. They struggled for more than five minutes to remove the painting from the double frames. The second time, experienced Louvre workers posed as the thieves and performed the same feat in moments.

The exercise suggested that someone skilled in museum work had separated Mona Lisa from her frames. The crime had been planned with precision and executed with skill. The thief—or thieves—had understood the internal operations of the Louvre, studied the layout of the museum, and laid out a clear strategy. They knew that the staircase where the frames were found, which was usually restricted, was accessible on Mondays. They also knew that the number of attendants would be at its lowest.

Suspicion pointed to an inside job. Prefect Lépine requested a complete list of everyone who had access to the museum between Sunday evening and Tuesday morning. No one was presumed innocent. Each custodian, curator, cleaner, workman, and photographer would be fingerprinted and interrogated.

4

THE FIRST TO FACE Judge Drioux in the judicial inquest was the guard Desornais, who should have been watching over Mona Lisa on Monday. He confessed reluctantly and with profuse apologies that Mona Lisa was alone from eight to ten o'clock Monday morning. Because the museum was closed to the public, only ten guards were on duty, and he had been covering the Grande Galerie, the Galerie d'Apollon, and the Salon Carré alone when he was called away to help move some paintings in another part of the museum. For those two hours on Monday morning, the entire area was unattended.

The next guard called was Paupardin, who had been on duty both Sunday and Tuesday. The old guard was still shaken, and he cradled his head in his hands. If he were able to see into the future, he would have paid closer attention, but a summer Sunday in the Louvre—who could remember?

Mon Dieu! The old guard bristled. *She was there when I left on Sunday night, when the museum closed. That is all I know.*

When Judge Drioux pressed for details, Paupardin could not be certain. It was difficult to recall anything about that day except the oppressive heat that had soaked through his uniform, through his vest, plastering it to his hairy chest.

Magistrate Drioux was known as "the bulldog" because of his tenacious, sometimes fierce questioning and a naturally churlish expression. Although the judge was not as ferocious as his dyspeptic appearance suggested, it was a deception that served him well. Under further probing, Paupardin remembered a group of young men, no more than three, all swarthy— dark hair, olive eyes, olive skin. He described them as *mangeurs de macaroni,* macaroni eaters, or the shorthand, "macaroni." Not typical museum visitors, the guard conceded, but well behaved. Orderly. Respectful.

Did one of them carry a package?

Paupardin had a fleeting memory of a flat brown paper parcel tied with string, but the men had not lingered.

Did they leave together? At what time?

Ah, yes, the time.

The questions continued, the judge pressing, a gendarme scribbling on lined paper, the demand for details becoming harsher. Judge Drioux's voice, coaxing at first, coarsened from smooth sand to gravel.

Paupardin had not paid close enough attention on Sunday to answer the questions fully, and he was growing defensive, fearful that he would be blamed for the loss. Paupardin did not volunteer that he had been less than watchful, dozing on and off for much of the afternoon, made drowsy by the midday cassoulet and the August heat. Nor did he regard it as essential to point out that he did not actually see any of the visitors leave the gallery.

But under intense questioning, Paupardin did recall a visitor who came to call often, as if paying court. The scent of oleander returned to the old guard, and he described in some detail the young man, German or maybe Austrian, as opaquely handsome as a marble statue, always neatly dressed, blond hair combed, slight but well proportioned, quiet, always alone, and always with eyes for only one. No words passed between them, only a bouquet.

I

Thursday, August 24

IN 1793, JUST STEPS FROM THE PLACE where Mona Lisa vanished, beautiful Charlotte Corday was sentenced to death for the assassination of the revolutionary theorist Jean-Paul Marat. Charlotte stabbed Marat in his bathtub and faced the guillotine with no regrets. She accepted her fate with such grace and courage that she captivated a romantic German student in the crowd of onlookers. Meeting her unflinching gray eyes, Adam Lux lost his heart and his head. He published a pamphlet denouncing her execution, and when he was arrested, he demanded to die as she had. He implored the Revolutionary Tribunal to send him to the same guillotine so their blood would mingle. He received his wish.

When *Le Matin,* one of the city's largest morning papers, reported that police were searching for a young German whose infatuation may have turned to obsession, Paris had a new Adam Lux. Prefect Lépine confirmed to reporters that the boy had visited Mona Lisa often enough for the guard in the Salon Carré to provide a detailed description. Curator of paintings Paul Leprieur added colorful embellishments. It was true that Mona Lisa often made men do strange things. There were more than one million artworks in the Louvre collection; she alone received her own mail. Mona Lisa received many love letters, and for a time they were so ardent that she was placed under police protection. The year before, a hopeless admirer, facing a lifetime of unrequited love, had shot himself in front of her.

A young man, and a German, crazed by love. It was the stuff of myth. In the popular press, the calculated crime was rewritten as a tender love affair. As news of the romance spread around the world, Mona Lisa became a passionate participant in her own disappearance. The *Chicago Tribune* entertained readers with a whimsical report of her elopement:

> *So Mona Lisa has another lover! Was it not enough that ... innumerable men should have seen in her face the eternal inscrutability of the feminine half of the world? ... Her portrait has been stolen, carried boldly from the Salon Carré ... she's gone. But may it not be by her own volition? ...*
>
> *Now, after four and a half centuries, Leonardo's subtle lady wins another lover, and her tantalizing discretion quite forgot, she flees with her wooer. Ten thousand dollars for her reward, cries Paris. Well, there was a Paris once who staked his country on a throw like that, and losing, counted the cost inadequate. ... Mona Lisa's innumerable lovers should unite to offer a purse that would bring her straightaway back to the place the world looks upon as her home. No one man should have exclusive right to feed on that mysterious loveliness.*

The fatal-attraction theory appealed to the French heart and softened the loss. If Mona Lisa was gone, at least she had been stolen for love.

2

AS THE INVESTIGATION entered its second day, every clue, however tenuous, was magnified. Every memory, every detail, took on significance and seemed to both freeze and meld, as if distinct art movements had converged on that summer day. The loss of the Renaissance masterpiece was recalled like an Impressionist painting. Parisians strolling along the quai or crossing the Pont des Arts that August Monday described a uniformed guard snoozing in front of the museum in the shade of a red umbrella.

A department store employee who was walking on the Quai du Louvre about seven-thirty a.m. had a vivid memory of a man with an odd gait and a bulky package under his arm, speeding toward the Pont du Carrousel. He was neither walking nor running but appeared to be moving at more of a canter along the Louvre side of the street. All at once and without slowing his pace, he tossed something small and shiny into the garden along the side of the museum. The witness could not say with certainty if the man continued on or turned to cross the bridge.

A second witness recalled a man, also carrying a bulky package, sweating profusely and rushing to catch the seven-forty express train for Bordeaux at the Gare d'Orsay. The glass-enclosed Beaux Arts terminal (now a museum) was just across the river from the Louvre. The seven-forty made fourteen stops on the nine-hour route from Paris to Bordeaux, and connecting trains could carry the thief out of the country as far as Madrid or Lisbon.

The two witnesses were painting the same clear picture until they began to describe the suspect. One recalled a trim middle-aged man of medium height, between forty and fifty, without hat or mustache. The other described a tall, heavyset man with a dark mustache, wearing a dark suit and a straw hat, in a state of extreme agitation.

Elements of each story were quickly corroborated. The Louvre's chief carpenter recalled passing through the Salon Carré with two new assistants at approximately seven o'clock, the start of their Monday shift. He pointed out Mona Lisa to them. When they returned around eight-thirty, she was gone, and he joked to the men, "Mona Lisa has been taken away for fear we would steal her."

A museum plumber named Sauve mentioned that a knob had been missing from the stairway door opening into the Cour du Sphinx—the same stairs where the frames were discovered. On Monday morning, Sauve had found a worker waiting at the foot of the stairs for someone to open the door. Sauve obliged, using his key and a pair of pliers to unlock it, and advised the other man to leave the door ajar so that no one else would be stuck. Police detectives raked through the garden behind the museum and retrieved a small, shiny object. It was a brass doorknob.

The plumber's behavior aroused suspicion. Sauve had not reported the missing doorknob until considerably later in the day, and he could not describe the other man clearly. The plumber was vague on every point except one: The man worked at the Louvre. He was wearing a white employee smock.

The brass doorknob raised as many questions as it answered. Why would the thief toss it into the garden where it would be easy to find? If he continued walking along the Quai du Louvre, why didn't he cross the street and drop the knob in the river? If he crossed the bridge, why didn't he drop it over the side? Mixing the descriptions of the two suspects like colors on a palette, Prefect Lépine dispatched an urgent bulletin to Bordeaux, but his direct authority ended at the outskirts of the capital.

France had two national police forces—the Préfecture de Paris, with jurisdiction over the city and its environs; and the Sûreté Nationale, responsible for maintaining law and order throughout the country. The Sûreté, under the direction of Inspector Octave Hamard, pursued leads and suspects beyond the Paris area. The two agencies were frequently in conflict. Hamard was a blustering man with an ample waist and a more than ample temper who still had the rough edges of a street cop. Lépine was as much a politician as a policeman. There was little rapport between them and little cooperation between the forces. Rivalry was inbred, and detectives from the two agencies guarded information and tried to discredit each other.

I

Friday, August 25

MONA LISA HAD THE most famous face in the world, and the most uncertain identity. Who was she? What was her relationship to Leonardo, and what was the secret of her smile? Generations of art historians had puzzled over her many aspects. Now there was an urgent new mystery to plumb: Where was she? Who took her, and most perplexing of all, why?

When Mona Lisa slipped out of her frames, she seemed to change from a missing masterpiece to a missing person. She came alive in the popular imagination. The public felt her loss as emotionally as an abduction or a kidnapping. Captivated by her mystery and romance, crowds gathered outside the Louvre each day, awaiting word from the prisonlike fortress that had failed to keep her safe. More people jammed Rue de Rivoli than ever visited the museum when it was open. Mona Lisa had always seemed *più vita che la vivacità*—more alive than life itself. The first description ever written of her said, "She does not appear to be painted, but truly of flesh and blood."*

One French paper after another promised generous rewards for her return. The popular weekly pictorial *L'Illustration* offered ten thousand francs ($40,000) for information and forty thousand francs ($160,000) if the painting were returned to the newspaper office, both good for one month, plus a bonus if the return was made by September 1. *L'Illustration* received more

---

* Giorgio Vasari.

than five hundred letters in a single day, and more than one hundred readers crowded the newsroom. The *Paris-Journal*, which also set a September 1 deadline, offered fifty thousand francs ($200,000) and a promise of anonymity to anyone who turned Mona Lisa in to the paper.

The government joined in with a reward of twenty-five thousand francs ($100,000). To angry and bereaved Parisians, it seemed a meager response to such a monumental loss. Henri Rochefort, a member of *les Amis du Louvre,* a group of wealthy museum patrons, told *Le Figaro,* "The Mona Lisa thief wants like all thieves to realize the price of his booty."* He proposed a campaign to raise one million francs ($400 million today), and he personally pledged to double the government's reward.

2

THE POLICE HAD THE FRAMES, a fingerprint, the date and approximate time of the theft, and a possible accomplice in the plumber Sauve, but they still had no idea how Mona Lisa had left the Louvre. She was not a canvas that could be rolled up and sneaked out of the museum or the country. Leonardo had painted her on a solid panel of white Lombardy poplar, twenty-one by thirty-one inches.

Mona Lisa would be difficult to conceal even without her frames, yet every exit guard insisted that she had not gone through his door. One attendant remembered stopping a workman with a wheelbarrow of trash around nine o'clock Monday morning and sifting through the debris. There was nothing

---

* In the end, the Friends of the Louvre set the reward at twenty-four thousand francs ($96,000).

resembling the painting in the barrow. Eight possible exits from the Louvre and eight firm denials from the guards. Mona Lisa was gone, but was she stolen? Was the vanishing act a crime or a hoax? Initial shock turned quickly to suspicion that the painting was still on the premises.

A few months before, a reporter had spent a night in a sarcophagus to expose lax security at the Louvre. A museum has no absolute defense against a cunning thief or sure protection against a crazed vandal, yet even allowing for the inherent difficulties, the art treasures of France were poorly guarded. Louvre security was casual at best. One hundred passkeys that unlocked every door in the museum were floating around the building. There was no alarm system. The most valuable works were not secured to the walls in any way. There was no surveillance over the photo process. Paintings were not signed in or out. And the Louvre was packed with political appointees.

Was Mona Lisa's disappearance a prank to dramatize the problem? Or were disgruntled Louvre workers settling scores? They had just won a bruising battle to unionize, and emotions were raw on both sides. Worse yet, were curators covering up an unforgivable crime? According to this scenario, the beautiful face had been disfigured in a botched effort at conservation. The evidence was stashed in the bowels of the museum, and after a suitable period of mourning, the true Leonardo would be replaced with a copy.

The Louvre is the largest museum in the world and an enormous labyrinth, covering some forty-nine acres. It is three times the size of the Vatican including St. Peter's Basilica, and its length is equivalent to two Eiffel Towers laid end to end. Rue de Rivoli is on one side, the River Seine on the other. Tourists roaming its halls with Karl Baedeker's *Paris and Its Environs 1910* would read that the picture galleries displayed three thousand paintings, including multiple Rembrandts, Raphaels, Titians, and six of the thirteen easel paintings by Leonardo da Vinci.

Searching the entire museum complex consumed an army of inspectors and gendarmes. They were combing every gallery, storage room, stairwell, and closet, even the vast underground vaults, filled with discarded splendors and fashioned from the caves of the ancient wolf hunters who gave the Louvre its name.* The search was proceeding meticulously, room by room, floor by floor.

Prefect Lépine vowed that if Mona Lisa were lost in the Louvre, his men would find her. Privately, though, he believed she was long gone. If the thieves had not used any of the exits, there was another possibility. A scaffold had been erected on the side of the museum where the first elevator was being installed. Although scrambling down scaffolding might not be the most ladylike means of egress, it offered an unguarded escape route.

3

FORTY-EIGHT HOURS AFTER Mona Lisa's absence was reported, there was still no demand for payment. If she was not a prisoner being held for ransom, the Paris picture magazine *L'Illustration* demanded to know, "What audacious criminal, what mystifier, what maniac collector, what insane lover, has committed this abduction? And where is the present abode of this marvelous picture?"

Paris had more newspapers than any other city in the world, and at least as many theories. In the pages of the Paris

---

* *Loup* + *vivre,* where wolves live.

press, the crime was condemned as an assault, a scandal, and an act of anarchy. The papers kept the story alive in the public imagination and the pressure on the police. They prodded the investigators, excoriated the museum administration and the government, and concocted their own outlandish scenarios.

The New York Times reported from Paris: "Feeling here about the affair is intense. An extraordinary number of absurd theories are advanced." Mona Lisa was stashed in the Louvre as a practical joke, to make a point, or to hide a blunder. She had been kidnapped by a madman. She had eloped with a desperate lover.

Reporters canvassed the opinions of art dealers and museum directors in France, England, and the United States. All gave the same answer. The painting was too famous to ever be sold on the art market for any price. No intelligent thief would take such a risk for a work he could never sell. But what if the thief did not intend to sell the painting?

An intriguing answer came from Joseph Reinach, a member of *les Amis du Louvre*. Paris in 1911 was both the incubator of a radical new art and a collectors' market for masterworks. Acquisitiveness and its offspring, forgery, were unrestrained. American magnates with a lust for old masters were competing with museums to buy the best art of Europe—and they were winning so often that a group of wealthy Frenchmen had organized the Friends of the Louvre to stanch the flow.

In an interview in *Le Temps,* Reinach said:

> *There are a great number of ancient, or alleged ancient, copies of* la Joconde. *I imagine that one or another of these copies has fallen into the hands of the authors of the theft. What would happen? Some weeks or some months from now, they will send to the Louvre the copy supposed to be the original, or they will even return the original, as the conservators of the Louvre could not be deceived a single instant by the*

most perfect copy. But they would sell the copy to the American millionaire collector, less skilled than the conservators, explaining that the picture they have for sale is the original and that the Louvre only possesses a copy.

Paris newspapers were highly partisan. So many were owned or operated by political groups that a distinction was drawn between "journals of opinion" and "journals of information." On both left and right, there was a suspicion that the balance of power in Europe had upset Mona Lisa from her secure spot in the Louvre.

Germany under the militaristic Kaiser Wilhelm II was expanding its navy, challenging Britannia's rule of the waves, and playing political chess in the Mediterranean, threatening French control of Morocco. Since July 1, when the German gunboat *Panther* reached the Moroccan port of Agadir, France and Germany had been edging toward war. It was a dangerous time for provocative games. The major European nations were bound by close alliances that compelled a collective response—Italy, Germany, and Austria in the Triple Alliance; France, Britain, and Russia in the Triple Entente. A threat to one was a threat to all.

Mona Lisa's disappearance was a conveniently timed distraction. "The news . . . has caused such a sensation that Parisians for the time being have forgotten the rumors of war," *The New York Times* reported.

Opposition parties suspected that the government had faked the theft to divert attention from the war threat. The timing seemed too perfect to be coincidence. The story was monopolizing the headlines, allowing time for tempers to cool and war to be postponed. An American in Paris, well connected in art circles, wrote home to his son: "One ingenious French friend told me confidentially that Mona Lisa was not stolen but it was an arrangement to serve as a new sensation for the public and press to divert attention from the German war scare and that the painting in time would turn up safe and sound."

Every political persuasion had a scenario. Nationalists suspected that Kaiser Wilhelm and his government had abducted a national treasure to humiliate France. Pro-Germans countered that the devious French had faked the theft not to distract from the war threat but to rouse sentiment against the kaiser.

When police in Bordeaux arrested a young German who matched the description of Mona Lisa's suitor, Germany lodged an official protest. The suspect had not been anywhere near Paris on August 21, and he was released within twenty-four hours. By then a second police incident was ruffling Franco-German relations. Acting on a report from detectives in Cherbourg, Prefect Lépine cabled New York that Mona Lisa was arriving in the United States on the North German Lloyd liner *Kaiser Wilhelm II*.

I

Saturday, August 26

EVERYONE HAD A THEORY, but no one had a clue.

Lépine was leaning toward the idea that a ring of expert art thieves was behind the abduction. The operation was too slick to be the work of a lovesick psychotic, a common crook, or any gang of amateurs, and it was too difficult for a single thief. Once Mona Lisa was removed from her frames, anyone could carry her easily, but with her double frames and protective glass, she weighed seventy-seven pounds (thirty-five kilograms).* Only a

---

* One quarter-inch protecting glass: twenty kg; box frame: two kg; gilded frame: five kg; painting: eight kg.

Goliath could have lifted her off the wall and maneuvered her to the stairway without accomplices.

Lépine appealed to the public for information on anyone seen in the vicinity of the Louvre on the morning of August 21. The response was overwhelming. Thousands sent letters or appeared in person at police precincts and newspaper offices to offer information, tips, or their own theories. If they had shown up in deerstalker hats and plaid cloaks, the desk sergeants and editors would not have been surprised.

Stories of brilliant amateur sleuths who solved cases that stumped the police were making detective fiction a popular new genre, and such favorite British series as Arthur Conan Doyle's Sherlock Holmes and G. K. Chesterton's Father Brown appeared regularly in French translation. When Mona Lisa vanished, everyone in France, it seemed, not just Alphonse Bertillon, became a Sherlock Holmes.

The public appeal produced few reliable clues but no shortage of cranks, nuts, and notoriety seekers. A University of London professor, whom the British press dismissed as an ornery iconoclast, railed that the stolen work was "one of the most actively evil pictures ever painted—the embodiment of all evil the painter could imagine put into the most attractive form he could devise."

A Sorbonne psychology professor warned in *Le Temps* that the thief might be a sexual psychopath who would treat Mona Lisa with "sadistic violence and fetishistic tendresse," take pleasure in "mutilating, stabbing and defiling" her, then return her when he was "through with her."

In *Le Figaro,* a historical novelist named Maurice Strauss fingered the infamous art thief Adam Worth, who had stolen Gainsborough's *Duchess of Devonshire* in 1876. "He has taken up the game again at our expense. The theft of *la Joconde* bears his signature," Strauss wrote. "There is only one man in the world who would have acted with such tranquil audacity and so much dexterity. It was Worth." The police were intrigued. Because the Gainsborough had eventually been recovered in America, U.S. customs officers increased security on the northern border, anticipating that Mona Lisa might be smuggled through Canada. There was one sticking point. Adam Worth had been dead for nine years.

Numerous letter writers claiming second sight recounted bizarre dreams that revealed where the painting was hidden. *Le Matin* enlisted two clairvoyants in the hunt and promised a reward "to anyone who by somnambulism, spiritualism or other occult means indicates the identity of the thief or the whereabouts of Mona Lisa." Gazing into her crystal ball, Madame Elise prophesied that the seductress had come to no good end—Mona Lisa had been destroyed. Madame Albanda da Silva, after studying the position of the planets at the time of the theft, swore that the painting was still in the Louvre, and she described the abductor as looking strangely like a bird, with a voice like a crow's, dark hair as fine as feathers, and an ostrich neck.

Tips poured in from all parts of Europe. Sûreté detectives were in Belgium following a tip that Mona Lisa was concealed in a freight train passing through Namur, Liège, and Brussels, en route to Holland. In León, two foreigners were arrested after the lady was discovered in their luggage. The men protested their innocence. They were tourists who had bought a copy of the missing painting as a souvenir. In Italy, a valuable Mona Lisa copy, painted during Leonardo's lifetime, was stolen from a luxurious villa on Lake Como.

In Calais, a slight, edgy man with a black mustache waxed at the tips took the Channel packet to Dover. He arrived in London, carrying all his worldly goods in a small- to medium-sized white wooden case, twenty-four by thirty-five inches, and appeared without an appointment at the Bond Street showroom of Duveen Brothers.

At a time when European art dealers were earning fortunes building collections for American tycoons, none were more powerful or successful than the Duveens. Brothers Joseph and Henry had a third clandestine partner, Bernard Berenson. A connoisseur and cultural snob, Berenson was a tiny man with a "tremendous excess of the 'I.'"* In his ambition to cultivate elegance and wealth, he acquired a Brahmin wife, the villa I Tatti in Florence, and a secret paymaster. For thirty years, Berenson was on the Duveens' books. The connoisseur and the dealers detested one another and made one another wealthy, profiting enormously from an alliance based on mutual greed and mistrust. As a team, no art brokers rivaled them. Duveen Brothers had offices in London, New York, and Paris. Profits were as high as 75 percent. In 1909 the Paris office alone realized $13 million (more than $290 million today).

Henry Duveen was in the Bond Street showroom when the stranger came in and insisted on seeing him alone and at once on "a very important matter." Duveen was immediately wary. He did not like the look of the man.

"Will you give me your word of honor that you will never reveal what I am going to tell you?" the man asked.

"Of course, of course," Duveen answered.

The dealer's brusqueness seemed to unnerve the man, and sidling closer, he whispered a warning. "If you don't, I and my friends will know how to deal with you. I have the *Gioconda* here in London. Will you buy it?"

The art broker was speechless. This stranger—"a seedy-looking foreigner," in Duveen's eyes—was the man police on three continents were hunting.

"Well, what do you say? What figure will you give me?" the man demanded.

* Leo Stein.

The Duveens had not become wealthy by being scrupulous. In the business of buying and selling art, a dubious provenance was no deterrence, but Henry Duveen wanted no part in such a sensational, highly publicized affair as the Mona Lisa heist. He did the first thing he could think of. He laughed as if he did not believe the story and walked away.

The stranger, dismissed so rudely in London, crossed the Channel again and made his way from Calais to northern Italy, where the American millionaire collector J. Pierpont Morgan was vacationing.

2

AMERICAN PORTS WERE ON HIGH ALERT. Customs officers, Pinkerton detectives, and Treasury Department agents were boarding every incoming ship that had made a port of call in France. In New York Harbor, they had searched the *Oceanic,* arriving from Southampton via Cherbourg with seven hundred passengers, and the *Provence,* which had departed from Le Havre.

Kaiser Wilhelm II was due to arrive in New York shortly. It had set out from Bremen, also making stops at Southampton and Cherbourg. Two suspects were listed on the ship's manifest. One was a New Yorker who embarked in Cherbourg, accompanied by a small, dark man. They were carrying two framed canvases with a wooden panel painting sequestered between them. French police had boarded the ship. The small man turned out to be a porter; the other was an American artist from the West Side of Manhattan. Although the paintings appeared to be his own compositions, the artist remained under suspicion.

The second suspect was a wealthy American dealer and

collector. His presence in Paris when the picture was stolen might have been coincidental, but he was a close student of Mona Lisa, and French police had kept him under surveillance since the theft.

When the *Kaiser Wilhelm II* docked in New York, customs officers went over the ship from stem to stern and inspected every piece of luggage. There was no trace of either Mona Lisa or the suspicious dealer-collector, but the investigation raised a new alarm in France: Was Mona Lisa smiling on an American millionaire?

3

ONCE THE FEAR WAS VOICED, sentiment deepened that such a vanishing act could only have been conjured by an American collector with the bravura, the wealth, the sense of entitlement, and the near-religious conviction that everything had a price.

The New York Times was soon reporting: "The belief is very general that the Florentine masterpiece is now in America. So certain is the press that *la Joconde* has gone to America, that articles are appearing . . . discussing the steps the French government would have to take to regain the national treasure if it had been smuggled across the ocean to America."

When Parisians said *"Cherchez l'Américain"*—Find the American—J. P. Morgan was the American they thought of first. If anyone had the aura of *droit du seigneur* to claim Mona Lisa for himself, it was Morgan. He was the gold standard of American millionaires. In the East Room of his mansion on Madison Avenue in New York (now the Morgan Library), a sixteenth-century Flemish tapestry hangs over the fireplace. The tapestry is called *The Triumph of Avarice.*

Morgan's own triumphs were legendary. Unlike most American tycoons, he did not have a Horatio Alger biography. Born to wealth and educated in Europe, Morgan had inherited millions, which he multiplied many times until he had more money than the U.S. Mint. Morgan was a one-man Federal Reserve before there was a Fed. When a national depression loomed, he bailed out the government, staving off a financial collapse. Ten years later, he did it again, and he still had ample funds to indulge his passion for collecting. Everything about him was impressive—his ambition, his art, his fortune, his physical size, his enormous eggplant nose (he suffered from a condition called rhinophyma), even the black cigars he chomped.

In the United States at the turn of the twentieth century, making money was an open game with few rules, and there was no income tax to cut into fortunes. For every J. P. Morgan or Andrew Mellon, raised in wealth and well educated, there were two or more self-made millionaires. H. E. Huntington started as a logroller. P. A. B. Widener was a butcher from Philadelphia. Samuel H. Kress made his fortune in the five-and-dime. Frick and Carnegie were coal men. The diffident bachelor Benjamin Altman parlayed a pushcart into a fashionable Fifth Avenue emporium. Each had his eccentricities. Altman never liked to buy a painting unless he could pronounce the artist's name. He had a weakness for Renaissance madonnas.

The art of Europe offered a coveted cachet of class, conferring instant pedigree and prestige on men who had none. Flattered to be taken as gentlemen to the manner born, they were easy prey for duplicitous dealers and cagy con men peddling both stolen works and "genuine fakes."* The Americans might be tough-nosed businessmen at home, but when they stepped off the gangplank in Cherbourg or Genoa, there were many waiting to take them by the hand and lead them down the

* Arabella Huntington.

proverbial garden path. James H. O'Brien, a businessman who was in Paris when Mona Lisa vanished, told *The Washington Post:* "Europeans look on Americans as good things. . . . They can spot Americans the moment they see them, and there's no use trying to masquerade. They go after you when you land and there is no escape."

The Americans, so clever at making money, were easily gulled to part with it. For the relatively modest sum of one million dollars, a Baltimore magnate named Henry Walters came home with an entire collection, including, he believed, eight Raphaels and half a dozen Titians that were purportedly the family heirlooms of the considerably less than noble Don Marcello Mazzarenti. Then there was the entertaining Guglielmo Kopp who, after much haggling, accepted $20,000 ($500,000 today) for *Trajan's Column* from an American railroad tycoon. Boasting that he had wrangled a bargain price, the American went home to the heartland to await delivery.

Unlike many who didn't know a da Vinci from a David, J. P. Morgan was an astute collector, but even he suffered an occasional fleecing. He was once persuaded to put a sizable down payment on the bronze doors of Bologna's Duomo di San Pietro, which has no bronze doors.

Morgan was vacationing in Italy when Mona Lisa disappeared, and there were persistent rumors that the thief had brought the painting to him. He had recently been caught with a stolen art treasure, the Cope of Ascoli, in his collection. A magnificent gold and silk vestment once worn by Pope Nicholas IV, the cope had been lifted from a cathedral in Italy. When its provenance was disclosed, Morgan donated the vestment to the Italian government. Parisians wanted him to do no less for Mona Lisa. Morgan had dealt with art thieves once. Why not again?

The press pursued him more relentlessly than the police were pursuing any other suspect. The Cope of Ascoli notwithstanding, Morgan resented the intimations that he would traffic in stolen goods and rebuffed the reporters. "I have not been offered Mona Lisa," he insisted, "and I regret it. Had it been offered, I should have bought it and given it back to France."

I

Sunday, August 27

MONA LISA HAD BEEN MISSING for less than a week, but the pressure to break the case and recover the painting was relentless. Everyone even tangentially involved tried to escape responsibility by pinning the blame on someone else. Police charged inept museum management. Museum administrators blamed government lassitude. The Ministry of Beaux Arts concluded its administrative inquest with a sharply worded criticism of the security at the national museums. The government needed a scapegoat, and the director of the Louvre was the obvious choice.

Jean Théophile Homolle, director of all the national museums of France, was a courtly man with a considerable reputation as an archaeologist and scholar. His specific area of expertise was ancient Greece, and in profile, his sharp, clean features resembled an Arcadian marble. But even if his head had been chiseled by Phidias, it would have rolled given the virulent climate in Paris.

Homolle had led the first archaeological dig at Delphi, and if he had been in Paris at the time of the theft, in all likelihood, one of the gossip sheets would have pictured him consulting the oracle for clues. But in the summer of 1911, he had traveled to the Yucatán Peninsula, where archaeologists were beginning to uncover the civilization of the Maya—a world reclaimed by the jungles long before Cortés reached Mexico. Homolle dug through the lost empire without any idea that his own world was disintegrating. One of the last to learn that Mona Lisa was missing, he was the first to pay for her disappearance.

In 1911, the perception of distance and time was changing. Horseless carriages and bicycles rolled down the grand boulevards of Paris. The first métro rumbled underground. A national railway network carried the Paris dailies to the provinces and brought the bumpkins to the big city. The Continental Train Bleu picked up English travelers in Calais and sped them to Paris, then on to Berlin and St. Petersburg. The eleven years from 1900 to 1911 saw the first flying machines, the first bus (called an autostage), the first moving pictures, and the first newsreel. A monoplane crossed the Channel successfully from Dover to Calais, and a balloonist tried unsuccessfully to cross the Atlantic.

Although telegraph, cable, and telephone were shrinking the gap between the time news was made and disseminated, the Yucatán jungle was beyond their reach. The urgent message dispatched by the minister of Beaux Arts to the director of the Louvre had to be relayed from Paris to New York to Havana to Veracruz, then by mule through the jungle to the base camp, and from there carried along narrow footpaths to the site of the dig. Homolle set out immediately on the arduous overland trek. The director and his team hacked their way through the overgrown forests down the steep, stony mountain. Monkeys cackled like a Greek chorus in the branches overhead.

Paris had its own outraged chorus of politicians, press, and public decrying the oversight at the Louvre. Although the porous security had been an open secret for years, the museum had either remained silent on the subject or had come up with bizarre solutions—such as training the old guards in judo or arming them like gendarmes with pistols, nightsticks, and whistles. Steps were finally being taken to address the problem.

The protective glass, much criticized, was one step, and additional security precautions, including a personal guard for Mona Lisa, were planned. Before leaving on vacation, Homolle had assured a skeptical press, with uncharacteristic bravura, that the Louvre was now secure. "You might as well pretend that one could steal the towers of the cathedral of Notre-Dame," he had boasted.

In the *avant-guerre* years, hyperbole would come back to haunt those who employed it. The *Titanic* was unsinkable, and the Louvre was impenetrable.

The *Paris-Journal* ran a photograph of Notre-Dame with one tower missing below the headline: COULD THIS HAPPEN TOO? *Le Figaro* deplored the lax security and denounced a government that "cannot guard the museum. Everything yet known about the theft shows a lamentable carelessness and extraordinary forgetfulness in the most elementary duties."

The best scholar doesn't always make the best administrator, and Director Homolle was far from blameless. The Louvre lacked the simplest precautions against theft, adopted decades earlier by other major museums. By 1853 the Uffizi Gallery was using safety hooks that locked the paintings in place, but not the Louvre. In an interview with the London *Times,* the British art critic M. H. Spielmann described a visit to Mona Lisa with Director Homolle as his guide:

> *He accompanied me most obligingly into the gallery, and we stood before the little picture. The light was bad so that it was difficult to see it. To my astonishment, my courteous host lightly lifted the work from the wall and held it for me to examine. I expressed my surprise, and asked if he had no fear of theft, adding that in London all our small pictures were firmly screwed into the walls.*
>
> *No, he explained, the Louvre was not built for a picture gallery; it was not fire-proof. . . . He lived in daily fear of fire,*

and regarded free and loose hanging as a precaution made
necessary in the circumstances. *

More shocking than the casual security was the lack of any coherent system of accountability. No one guarded the paintings taken to the photo studios or supervised the photographers. Even more incredibly, the Louvre required no authorization to take a painting from a gallery. In Britain and Germany, if a painting were removed, a notice was posted in the empty space explaining why the work was missing and when it would return. According to Homolle's policy or lack of one, a photographer could move any painting to the museum studio and keep it indefinitely without a word to anyone.

After eight years as director of the national museums of France, Homolle was tried in the press. The *Revue Bleue* charged "anarchy at the Louvre." The international press echoed the criticism, reporting that "chaos reigned supreme." "The Director on account of political trammels could not direct, the trustees neglected their trust, and a totally inadequate number of ill-paid, unruly and shiftless custodians were entirely incompetent to watch over the priceless treasures entrusted to them."[†]

Homolle was figuratively dragged from the Louvre to the Place de la Concorde; it remained only for the guillotine blade to fall. Four days later, on August 31, in a special meeting of the cabinet of government ministers, he would be denounced as "a savant devoid of administrative ability" and indicted for failing to safeguard the national treasure. Homolle would be fired, and the ministers would appoint as interim director Eugene M. Pujalet, inspector general of administrative services.

---

* This visit occurred before the painting was placed in a boxed frame.
[†] *Bookman* magazine, 1911.

Though far from blameless, Homolle was not the source of the trouble. The Louvre's problems were systemic. The museum had become a dumping ground, staffed with inept cronies and hangers-on. Politicians used museum positions for patronage jobs. Given the sensationalism of the case, politics inevitably intruded. The ultranationalist newspaper *Action Française* stoked the anti-Semitism that had been stirred by the Dreyfus Affair, the case against Alfred Dreyfus, an army captain and a Jew falsely charged with treason and imprisoned on Devil's Island:

> The Republic of the Jews has transformed the museum into a bazaar. Homolle, who has been sacked, was in their pockets. The regime is the cause of the loss of the *Joconde,* gloriously acquired by our kings, and part of our national heritage since François I.

Italy joined the war of words, expressing umbrage that a beautiful, innocent Italian woman had been left unprotected by France. With great fanfare, the Italian ambassador Tommaso Tittoni, who was also president of the Society of Italian Artists in Paris, led a pilgrimage to Leonardo's burial spot at Amboise in the Loire valley. Speaking with passion and eloquence, the ambassador pronounced, "Leonardo da Vinci belongs to Italy by birth, to France by his mortal remains, to the world by art."

I

Monday, August 28

THE SEARCH OF THE LOUVRE WAS COMPLETE. The initial flurry of success had raised hopes, but the investigation had not advanced materially since then.

While Lépine's men had been scouring the museum, in one of the world's first forensic crime laboratories—a cramped space in the eaves of the Palais de Justice on Île de la Cité—Alphonse Bertillon had spent the week meticulously comparing fingerprints with the impression he had lifted from Mona Lisa's box frame. In an adjoining room, the plumber Sauve had been sweating through piles of mug shots, trying to find the face on the stairs. Neither search was successful. Sauve had not paid close enough attention to the man to make an identification. Bertillon had compared the fingerprints of more than two hundred Louvre employees, from curators to custodians, and had found no match.

After the frames, the fingerprint, and the doorknob, nothing more was found, not a trace of the picture or the thief, not a single clue. All current and former museum employees, going back five years, were being deposed, but interrogating witnesses was like trawling in the Seine: So much sewerage was dredged up that it was difficult to separate the valuable nuggets from the sludge. Museum workers were reluctant to answer fully and candidly, hampering the investigation. Premature threats of punishment and dismissal had roused a spirit of resistance. They feared recrimination and resented the slur on their integrity. As the attendants grew more defensive, the interrogators grew more impatient.

2

A WEEK AFTER locking its doors, the Louvre was preparing to reopen and expose the naked wall to the public. The judicial inquiry would continue, but it was moving to the Palais de Justice. Magistrate Drioux issued an interim report that underscored how little progress had been made. After six days, countless interrogations, depositions, and false leads, he could state only two facts "with certitude": 1) Mona Lisa was no longer in the Louvre; 2) the theft was premeditated and "executed with unequaled audacity." The judge could say "almost certainly" that the thief had spent the night of Sunday, August 20, concealed in the museum and had left with Mona Lisa through the Porte Visconti. "From that point," he conceded, "we lose all trace of the thief. . . . His movements have been a complete mystery."

The floundering investigation was a very public embarrassment for the two chief investigators. Alphonse Bertillon and Louis Lépine did not have the rapport of a Holmes and Watson. Their relationship was pragmatic, but they needed each other, and they needed to solve the case.

Bertillon's motive was personal. He was fifty-eight, although he appeared many years older, and not an easy man to warm to. Aloof and acerbic, too intelligent to suffer fools, he had few equals and fewer friends. It was said that he treated criminals with courtesy and his colleagues with scorn. For Bertillon, *l'Affaire de la Joconde* was an opportunity to restore his reputation, which had been damaged in the bitter Dreyfus Affair. Bertillon had testified as an expert witness against the captain, swearing under oath that falsified documents were authentic, and he had refused to correct his testimony, even after Dreyfus was retried and proved innocent.

Lépine's motive was professional. "The most colossal art theft in history" had been committed under his nose, within his jurisdiction. The loss might be blamed on the casual security at the Louvre, but the recovery was his charge. He had promised a speedy return, and so far he had failed to deliver. Although the investigation was still in its first week, the police were allowed no grace period. The clamor for answers was relentless, and the sacrifice of Director Homolle was not enough to silence the critics.

From the outset, problems had complicated the investigation. Given the Louvre's laissez-faire attitude toward security and record keeping, simply compiling a complete and accurate list of everyone with a Monday pass proved impossible. Even with the reduced staff, as many as eight hundred people could have been working in the museum or wandering through the galleries at any point on the day of the theft. The initial list given to the police contained only two hundred fifty-seven names.

Even more damaging to the investigation was the late start. By the time the police were alerted, the thieves had made a clean getaway. The Gare d'Orsay was just steps from the Louvre, and the port of Le Havre was within easy reach. With at least a twenty-four-hour head start, Mona Lisa could have crossed the border in any direction before she was missed.

Prefect Lépine continued to believe that a ring of skilled art thieves was behind the abduction, but he was no closer to flushing out the gang than he was on the first day, and he found the lack of a plausible motive baffling. As he said, "It is generally conceded that even a dull person would realize the impossibility of selling such a famous work."

The *Paris Herald* expressed his frustration:

Though the police and detectives inquiring into the theft of Mona Lisa continue as active as ever, all the clues followed so far have ended in complete failure, and the whereabouts of the masterpiece remain as deep a mystery as ever.

THE BLANK WALL

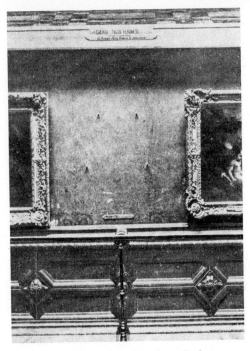

When the Louvre reopened a week after
Mona Lisa vanished, a record number of visitors came
to the museum to view the empty space.

(Courtesy of Mary Evans Picture Library)

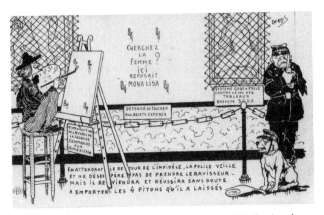

The leading political cartoonist in France, an artist who signed
himself "Orens," satirized *l'Affaire de la Joconde.* A painter is copying
the empty pegs where Mona Lisa once hung for an American collector,
while the chicken wire over the remaining paintings, the elderly guard,
and the little dog mock the new Louvre security measures.

(Courtesy of Musée de la Carte Postale, Antibes, France)

I

MONA LISA BECAME the most wanted woman in the world. Eleven years after Guglielmo Marconi sent the first wireless message from England to Newfoundland, her story was flying around the world. *L'Illustration* wrote, "The entire world shares the stupefaction of Paris over Mona Lisa's disappearance." Each new development—and each disappointment—in the unfolding case made news. To a significant extent, the rise of a popular press with the power to direct public opinion drove the case, influencing and at times impeding the police investigation.*

Between 1890 and 1914, newspaper readership nearly tripled. More people could read because elementary education had become mandatory, and more people wanted to read because the newspapers had become more appealing. This was the golden age of popular journalism, when wars were reported as glorious adventures and crimes of passion were rewritten as Romeo and Juliet romances with a salaciously sinister edge. The boom was born in America in the 1880s, when William Randolph Hearst, Jr., the youthful publisher of the *San Francisco Chronicle,* moved east to compete in the huge New York market for influence and readers. Soon Hearst's *New York*

---

* The first radio programming for the French public did not begin until December 1921. Radiola, the first private radio station in France, began to broadcast in 1922.

Journal was taking on the *New York World,* flagship of the reigning media king Joseph Pulitzer. In the newspaper wars they waged, competition was cutthroat, facts were incidental, and boundaries of truth and taste were trampled. The goal was to form, more than inform, public opinion. Sensational stories sold papers—the more sensational, the higher the circulation.

The technologies of the emerging age—photo reproduction and Marconi's wireless—propelled the story of the vanished Mona Lisa far beyond the country's borders. Print journalism had always been all type, no pictures.* The development of commercial photography, beginning around 1880, changed that. Photogravure and other mechanical printing techniques replaced the laborious, time-consuming process of engraving and lithography, opening visual culture to mass consumption.

When *Le Petit Parisien* introduced illustrated supplements in France in the 1880s, circulation jumped. Now with more than a million readers, it claimed to be the largest daily newspaper in the world—and it was just one of a dozen major dailies in Paris with a national circulation. Where it had taken thousands of extravagant words to describe a single picture, almost overnight, a picture became worth a thousand words. As photography developed into a popular medium, illustrated books, calendars, and billboards proliferated, and pictures became a common household accessory. Sunday editions capitalized on the popularity of illustrations, adding funny papers and picture inserts.

Luigi Calamatta, a skilled artisan, spent twenty years, from 1837 to 1857, making the first exact engraving of Mona Lisa. Now, in a matter of days, her photograph was seen in every world capital. More people recognized Mona Lisa than the president of France. In New York, a Bloomingdale's ad offered: "Copies of the famous painting *Mona Lisa* or *La*

---

* Before photography, there were occasional sketches and caricatures.

Joconde, Da Vinci's masterpiece which mysteriously disappeared from its place in the Louvre Museum of Paris, now at Bloomingdale's Picture Store, 3rd floor, at 25 cents. Larger copies of *Mona Lisa,* exquisitely framed, at $9.98."

NOT SO LONG BEFORE, Mona Lisa had been just another pretty face in the Louvre collection. Her estimated value was significantly less than many Raphaels, and works by Murillo, Correggio, Titian, and Veronese were copied twice as often. When nineteenth-century Romantics began to idealize her as a dangerously alluring femme fatale, the essential Eve, in all her innocence and intrigue, her fortune changed. To Renaissance artists, Mona Lisa represented an extraordinary technical achievement. To the Romantics, she posed a tantalizing psychological puzzle. The dichotomy of Madonna and whore, mother and temptress, seductress and seduced stirred the romantic imagination.

As her mystique deepened, many came to pay her court— passionate art historians, lovesick suitors, and ardent critics. They saw, in her eternal beauty, infinite depth and dangerous enchantment. Never has so much been read into so few inches.* Mona Lisa's new fame quickly eclipsed every other work. In 1850 she was Number 1601 in the Louvre's catalog of paintings—one among many admired works in the collection. The 1878 Baedeker described her with some restraint as "the most celebrated work of Leonardo in the Louvre." By 1910 Baedeker was calling her "the most celebrated female portrait in the world, the sphinx-like smile of which has exercised the wits of generations of poets and artists and still fascinates in spite of the darkened condition of the canvas [*sic*]."

---

* Artists were as besotted as poets. In the 1840s, Aimée Brune-Pages's canvas *Leonardo Painting the* Mona Lisa sold for two thousand francs, a high price.

Now global attention lifted her out of the museum, the preserve of the elite, and brought her to an audience that knew little or nothing about the Renaissance or its idiosyncratic genius. Leonardo had been a shameless self-promoter in life. In a letter of introduction to the Duke of Milan, the young da Vinci wrote:

> I have sufficiently seen and examined the inventions of all those who count themselves makers and masters of instruments of war, and I have found that in degree and operation their machines are in no way different from those in common use. I, therefore, make bold, without ill-will to any, to offer my skills to Your Excellency, and to acquaint Your Lordship with my secrets, and will be glad to demonstrate effectively all these things, at whatever time may be convenient to you.

Four hundred years later, he was again the center of attention. His Mona Lisa had always exerted an extraordinary attraction on the titled and the talented. The theft and the sustained international attention made her a masterpiece for the masses—a phenomenon of a new popular culture, both persuasive and pervasive.

The painted lady who exerted such intriguing power over flesh-and-blood men was an instant international sensation. Hearst and Pulitzer had created news extravaganzas before, but the hoopla was for home consumption. Only wars had received such extensive worldwide coverage. Mona Lisa's disappearance was a global media event. *L'Affaire de la Joconde* combined beauty and loss, mystery and money, with hints of lust and romantic obsession. Millions of newspaper readers were beguiled.

James O'Brien, the San Francisco businessman, wrote home:

Paris is Mona Lisa crazy. When it was discovered that the famous painting was gone, the papers got out extras and there was more excitement about it than there was about the negotiations between France and Germany. . . . The newsboys looked upon me as a crazy person when I refused to buy their papers. I had suggested that I didn't even know Mona Lisa.

Like O'Brien, most newspaper readers had never been inside the Louvre or glimpsed the lost Leonardo. Now her face was as familiar as a friend's or lover's.

Newspapers in a dozen countries plumbed the mystery of her life and loves with unabashed poetic license. Mona Lisa was not the most glamorous face in France, but she was the biggest boost to circulation. Millions of readers who had never heard of her seven days before were glued to every installment of the missing person story.

The Renaissance masterwork became the people's painting—the lost love of the nation and the world. Obituaries were written for the elusive woman who had come to symbolize all women. Novenas and Masses were offered, and the masses mourned.

2

PARISIANS HAD EXPECTED a swift recovery: the hoax exposed, a ransom quietly paid, the lady returned unharmed. Instead, the reopening of the Louvre became a national wake. On Tuesday morning, August 29, thousands of grieving Parisians lined up to view the blank space on the gallery wall. *Le Figaro* described it as "an enormous, horrific, gaping void" and reported that "the crowds didn't look at the other paintings. They contemplated at length the dusty space where the divine Mona Lisa had smiled the week before."

A cordon of four gendarmes and six museum guards stood at attention as the mourners and the merely curious filed past the blank wall and paid their respects to the emptiness. Detectives in plainclothes mingled with the crowd. The darkened rectangle with the four vacant iron pegs became the empty casket of a missing person. The mourners left flowers and notes, wept, and set new attendance records. There had never been a wait to enter the Louvre. Now the lines stretched for blocks.

The capitals of Europe had long been the exclusive domain of upper-crust visitors, but the faces of the crowds were changing. The Cook's Tour was competing with the Grand Tour. Sorrowful Parisians, rubes from the provinces, and foreigners from many continents congregated outside the museum—émigré artists intent on revolution, unemployed "macaroni" with nothing better to do, Greeks and Turks side by side, eccentric British ladies of an uncertain age and young English lords touring the Continent, Cook's tourists from America seeing Paris for the first time, Negroes from Morocco, and Cossacks from the steppes of Russia, students from the low countries, and American tycoons in the market for prestige and paintings. The *Paris Herald* described it as "an invading crowd. All classes and conditions of men and women mounted the stairway like a crowd hurrying into a big railway station."

Among those who stood in line to pay their respects were two young Germans, Max Brod and his friend Franz Kafka, both aspiring writers, on summer vacation. They had been to Zurich and Lugano and were ending in Paris. Traveling with little money had given them a bright idea. They would write a series of guidebooks—*On the Cheap in Switzerland, On the Cheap in Paris*. They imagined making their fortunes.

In Paris, they were swept up in the excitement of the lost

Leonardo. She was nowhere in the Louvre, but she was everywhere else, smiling from kiosks, advertisements, and magazine covers. An avant-garde movie short, *Nick Winter et le vol de la Joconde,* spoofed the tumult over the theft. Kafka and Brod went to see the film.

In the five-minute slapstick comedy, the only clue is a shoe button. To follow the lead, Detective Nick Winter disguises himself as a shoeshine boy and forces everyone to submit to a polish. Between the chaos at the Louvre and the frenzied polishing, no one notices when the thief returns with Mona Lisa, then slips away again with a Velásquez. Everyone involved in the case is myopic, including the thief, but he is thoughtful enough to leave a note: "Sorry, blame my poor eyesight. I wanted the picture next to her."

Mona Lisa's theft has been called the "perfect crime of the Modernist era"* because it seemed to mirror the nihilism that would preoccupy the new century. Although the lost painting was a masterpiece of the Renaissance, the blank space conveyed the message of modern art—the void at the heart of Western civilization.

Thousands stood and gazed at nothingness, absorbing absence. They contemplated, in sorrow and seriousness, what was not there. In a way, it should have been a triumph for the young Turks of the new art. Instead, it was almost their downfall.

3

ON AUGUST 29, the day the museum opened its doors again, a "canary" began to sing. He did not chirp softly into the ear

---

* Darian Leader, *Stealing the* Mona Lisa.

of Prefect Lépine or Magistrate Drioux but sang loudly and publicly to the editors of the *Paris-Journal*. It was not a random choice. Although several major newspapers were advertising rewards, the *Paris-Journal* offered the most generous money and a promise of anonymity. The *Journal* had an additional advantage: Its arts editor, André Salmon, was a friend of the informer.

As the Louvre reopened, the *Paris-Journal* devoted its front page to a startling confession.

A THIEF BRINGS US A STATUE STOLEN FROM THE LOUVRE

CURATOR ADMITS THE PIECE IS FROM THE MUSEUM.

AN EDIFYING STORY—OUR MUSEUM IS A SUPPLY CENTER FOR UNSCRUPULOUS INDIVIDUALS

The arresting headline ran with an unusual note from the editors. It identified "The Thief" as "a young man, aged somewhere between twenty and twenty-five, very well mannered, with a certain American chic, whose face and look and behavior bespoke at once a kind heart and a certain lack of scruples." In exchange for two hundred fifty francs ($1,000), the Thief sold the *Journal* a small statue he had filched from the museum and made a full confession, which the paper played verbatim on page one:

> It was in March, 1907, that I entered the Louvre for the first time—a young man with time to kill and no money to spend. At that time, I had no idea of ever "working" in the museum. . . .
> It was about 1 o'clock. I found myself in the gallery of Asiatic antiquities. A single guard was sitting motionless. . . .

*The place impressed me profoundly because of the deep
silence and the absence of any human being. I walked through
several adjoining rooms, stopping now and again in a dim
corner to caress an ample neck or well-turned cheek.*

*It was at that moment that I suddenly realized how easy it
would be to pick up and take away almost any object of moderate size.*

The Thief went on to explain how he had chosen the head of
a woman, concealed it under his vest, and walked out. He sold
the statue to a Parisian painter-friend for fifty francs ($200),
which he lost the same night in a billiard parlor.

*"What of it?" I said to myself. "All Phoenicia is there for the
taking."*

*The very next day I took a man's head with enormous
ears—a detail that fascinated me. And three days later, a
plaster fragment covered with hieroglyphs. A friend gave me
twenty francs for this last. I stole it from the large room
adjoining the Phoenician room.*

Then I emigrated.

*I made a little money in Mexico, and decided to return to
France and form an art collection at very little expense. Last
May 7th I . . . took the head of a woman, and stuffed it in my
trousers. . . .*

*And now one of my colleagues has spoiled all my plans for
a collection by making this hullabaloo in the painting department! I regret this exceedingly, for there is a strange, an
almost voluptuous charm about stealing works of art, and I
shall probably have to wait several years before resuming my
activities.*

4

THE NEXT DAY, Wednesday, August 30, the paper reported a second encounter with the Thief. The page-one report read:

> *We had a visit—a business visit this time—from The Thief who, after pocketing the agreed ransom, handed us a sheet of paper on which he had written this amusing protest:*
>
> *"To the Editor in Chief:*
>
> *"In an age when the right of REPLY is universally recognized by the press, you will allow me a few words of protest against certain terms of abuse leveled at me in your issue of yesterday, relative to the theft of the Phoenician statuette. A professional thief, lacking all moral sense, would remain unaffected by them; but I am not without sensitivity, and the few pilferings I have engaged in have been caused by momentary 'difficulties.' Bourgeois society, which makes life so hard for anyone without funds, whatever his intellectual qualities, is responsible for these wanderings from the straight and narrow."*

The note was signed Baron Ignace d'Ormesan.

At the request of the newspaper, Louvre curator Bénédite examined the statue and confirmed that it was Louvre property. Only the attribution was false. The statue was Iberian, not Phoenician, as the Thief believed. It had been stolen from an exhibit of pre-Christian artifacts in the museum. Bénédite not only validated the statue's authenticity, he admitted that the Thief's story was probably accurate.

The recovered figure went on display in the window of the *Paris-Journal,* and hundreds jammed the newspaper office to view the stolen art. *L'Affaire des Statuettes* was a huge coup

for the paper. In Paris of 1911, there were virtually no sub-
scriptions or home delivery. Since readers bought their newspapers each day from the corner kiosk, the most arresting
headline or a continuing story that kept them coming back day
after day for the next installment sold the most newspapers.
L'Affaire des Statuettes had both.

The next day, the *Paris-Journal* flaunted its success with
another page-one story:

> *The visitors to our windows exchanged many comments, and
> we shall spare the officials of the French Government any
> repetition of the litany of vigorous remarks addressed in their
> direction. So many cameras—both still and motion-picture—
> were aimed at the bust that the enigmatic Mona Lisa might
> almost have been jealous.*

The *Paris-Journal* printed more papers than ever before,
and the press runs sold out as soon as a new edition hit the
street. The newspaper played the story to the hilt, jabbing the
police and the government. On the road again, his pockets full
of francs, the Thief continued his mischief-making, writing to
the paper from various towns.

His next dispatch—headlined A PLEA FROM OUR THIEF
TO HIS "COLLEAGUE"—was a mocking thank-you:

> *I do not want to leave France without once again sending
> you my thanks for the chivalrous manner in which you han-
> dled the little matter in which I was concerned. And I hope
> with all my heart that the Mona Lisa will be returned to you.
> I am not counting very heavily on such an event. However, let
> us hope that if its present possessor allows himself to be
> seduced by the thought of gain, he will confide in your news-
> paper, whose staff has displayed toward me such a praise-
> worthy degree of discretion and honor. I can only urge the
> person at present holding Vinci's masterpiece to place himself*

entirely in your hands. He has a colleague's word for it that your good faith is above all suspicion.

Adieu! I am about to leave France, to finish my novel.—
Baron Ignace d'Ormesan.

There was a rueful sort of chivalry and irreverent humor in these missives to the *Paris-Journal,* but the French police were not amused. The "baron" reveled in being the center of the biggest story in France and was leaving a trail as deliberately as Hansel and Gretel.

For the first time since Mona Lisa vanished, Parisians had cause to be optimistic. Prefect Lépine believed that the same ring of international art thieves was behind both Louvre thefts—*l'Affaire des Statuette*s and *l'Affaire de la Joconde.* If he could collar the baron and his colleagues, the hunt would be over and the lost Leonardo would return to the Louvre. The print had barely dried on the morning paper when Lépine's men had compiled a complete dossier on Baron Ignace d'Ormesan. *Le Petit Parisien* reported: "The police now have a real clue to the thief of *la Joconde.*"

The notorious Mona Lisa thieves were not the usual suspects.

NOT THE USUAL SUSPECTS

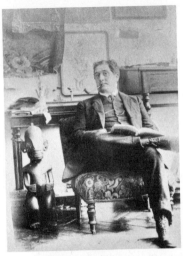

APOLLINAIRE IN PICASSO'S
STUDIO
Shortly after moving from
le bateau-lavoir to a new
studio-apartment on Boulevard
de Clichy, Picasso photographed
Apollinaire there.
(Courtesy of Réunion des Musées
Nationaux/Art Resource, New York.
© ARS, New York/Musée Picasso)

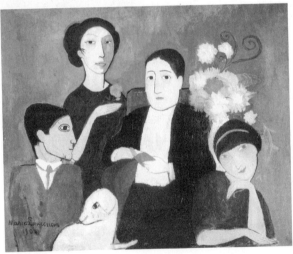

PAINTING BY MARIE LAURENCIN, *GROUP OF ARTISTS*, 1908
The prime suspects were as shocking as the heist—two young Turks
of the modern art movement, the poet Guillaume Apollinaire and the
painter Pablo Picasso. The Paris police suspected they were ringleaders
of an international gang of art thieves. Shown here with their
"molls" are (left to right) Picasso; Fernande Olivier; Apollinaire,
looking oddly like Gertrude Stein; and Marie Laurencin, who painted the
"gang of four." Marie sold the work to Gertrude Stein. It was her first sale.
(Marie Laurencin, French, 1885–1956. *Group of Artists,* 1908; oil on canvas, 25½ × 31¼ inches
(64.8 × 81 cm.). The Baltimore Museum of Art: The Cone Collection, formed by
Dr. Claribel Cone and Miss Etta Cone of Baltimore, Maryland, BMA 1950.215.

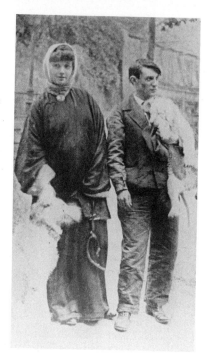

PICASSO AND FERNANDE
Picasso and Fernande Olivier,
his first mistress-muse, in
Montmartre in 1906. Picasso
would call this youthful period the
happiest years of his life.
(Courtesy of Réunion des Musées
Nationaux/Musée Picassso/
Art Resource, New York)

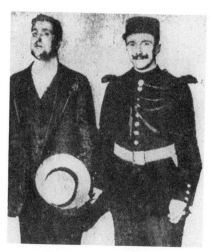

APOLLINAIRE IN HANDCUFFS
Apollinaire, arrested and in
handcuffs, is brought before Judge Drioux.
Apollinaire felt publicly humiliated by his ordeal.

I

IN A SUMMER OF UNUSUALLY HOT DAYS, September 2 was a record-breaker. In Paris, the temperature exceeded ninety-seven degrees, and four people died. But the arts editor of the *Paris-Journal,* André Salmon, remained cool. He spent the morning closeted in his office with detectives from the Paris Prefecture, who were demanding information on Baron d'Ormesan. Salmon's rebuff was courteous and couched with sincere regrets. He was bound by professional ethics not to reveal his sources.

The investigation of the Louvre thefts was turning as hot as the weather. The front page of the *Paris Herald* announced: POLICE MAY HAVE CLUE TO MISSING *MONA LISA*. Prefect Lépine hinted that a "*coup de théâtre*" was imminent. Although Alphonse Bertillon's criminal records turned up no information on Baron Ignace d'Ormesan, he was a familiar name to the Parisian literati. D'Ormesan was a fictional character in *L'Hérésiarque et cie,* a collection of stories nominated for the country's most prestigious literary award, le Prix de Goncourt. The police were soon knocking on the apartment door of the baron's very real, very voluble creator, Guillaume Apollinaire.

In the seven years from 1905 through 1911, the genesis story of modern art was being written. Pablo Picasso was its genius; Guillaume Apollinaire was its impresario. A flamboyant poet and cultural provocateur, he enunciated the modernist creed, adopting the Marquis de Sade's maxim "In art, one has to kill one's father." What Ezra Pound was to poets, Apollinaire was to painters. He was their catalyst, theoretician, and evangelist. Urging the destruction of all museums "because they paralyze the imagination," he championed Picasso "as a young god who wants to remake the world."

Never one to avoid an argument or keep an opinion to himself, Apollinaire had been uncharacteristically silent since Mona Lisa's disappearance. Although it was the most sensational story of the summer and he was a frequent and prolific contributor to many publications, he wrote only one article about the theft. In a column in the paper *L'Intransigeant* three days after the disappearance, Apollinaire praised the painting and damned the museum:

> *The Mona Lisa was so beautiful that her perfection has come to be taken for granted. There are not many works of which this can be said. But what shall we say of "The guard that watches the gates of the Louvre"?*
>
> *The pictures, even the smallest, are not padlocked on the walls, as they are in most museums abroad. Furthermore, it is a fact that the guards have never been drilled in how to rescue pictures in case of fire. The situation is one of carelessness, negligence, indifference.*

Apollinaire's declaiming against a museum was nothing new. He had signed a manifesto that threatened to "burn down the Louvre." But complimenting Mona Lisa was a surprise and an about-face. As the crown jewel of the Louvre collection Mona Lisa had become a symbol of the stale museum art that, the avant-garde believed was stifling new ideas and new talent. She was the archetype of the dead masterpieces they were rejecting and an obvious target for their attacks.

Apollinaire and Picasso were in the vanguard of the impassioned battles being waged in Paris over the direction of the

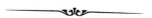
arts. They were friends and leaders of a group loosely known as *la bande de Picasso*. Familiar from Montmartre to Manhattan as "the Wild Men of Paris,"* Picasso's gang of painters and poets were the outlaws of traditional art, riding into town like the cowboys of the Wild West to slay the Renaissance gods. Young, brilliant, and ruthlessly ambitious, they strutted through the cobblestone streets of Montmartre and filled the cheap cafés, defining themselves as well as a new creative idiom, breaking the rules to free art from art history. Much of their art and their antics were "shocks of discovery"† committed to roil the status quo. More has been written about Bloomsbury, the London-based group of artists and writers, though it was less expansive and more inbred—a hothouse where *la bande de Picasso* was a wild garden. Passions were rude and rowdy. Ideas had the power to shock, and epiphanies came thick and fast.

After two frustrating weeks, Lépine believed he had cracked the case. In *la bande de Picasso* he had found the international ring of art thieves he had been hunting. Lépine was convinced that Apollinaire was one of the nefarious "colleagues" the baron had implicated in the Mona Lisa heist—"making this hullabaloo in the painting department."

To the police, the case was persuasive. Seizing the Mona Lisa was an insolent act in what Apollinaire called "the endless quarrel between Order and Adventure." It was a declaration of independence. What more dramatic way to kill your father than to target the most famous painting by the most provocative Renaissance master?

The Picasso "gang" had been lionized as romantic renegades. When the police identified them as a ring of "foreign thieves and swindlers who had come to France to plunder its treasure," escapades once excused as careless exuberance

* "The Wild Men of Paris," *Architectural Review,* May 1910.
† Jean Cocteau.

assumed sinister overtones. Tales circulated of the Picasso gang's coming back from the cafés of Montmartre late at night, frequently drunk, shouting, singing, and declaiming in the squares. Picasso always carried a Browning, and he would wake up the neighbors by shooting it into the charged air.

Stunned by the greatest art theft in history, Paris was shocked anew to learn that the prime suspects were the firebrands of the modern-art movement.

2

THE VILLAGE OF CÉRET squats against the high Pyrenees on the French side of the border. Its spirit is Catalan, its cuisine is French, which made Céret the perfect marriage for the expatriate Spanish painter and his group of poets, artists, and amours. They had arrived in the remote village early in August bearing life's few essentials: rolls of canvas, sketchbooks, oils, inks, and a portable paraffin stove. After commandeering the entire first floor of the Hôtel du Canigou, they settled in for the summer to invent cubism. Picasso arrived first in mid-July; Braque followed in August. Later, he would say that he and Picasso had worked so closely they "were roped together like mountaineers."

The Paris papers came late to Céret,* so the vacationers were always two or three days behind the news. Over morning coffees enjoyed in midafternoon, they caught up with accounts of the heist with an air of bemused detachment. The *Paris-Journal* arts editor André Salmon was their friend and neighbor, and they suspected his ironic pen in the early articles on

---

* Picasso wrote to Apollinaire on the 24th about an article he had read that same morning in *Le Matin*. The story ran in the August 22 paper.

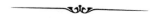
l'Affaire de la Joconde. That the Louvre was a sieve was not news to them, and they had no sympathy for it. They dismissed museums as "graveyards of history."

"We have infected the pictures in museums with all our mistakes, all our poverty of spirit," Picasso would say. "We have turned them into petty and ridiculous things. We have been tied up to a fiction, instead of trying to sense what inner life there was in the men who painted them."

Among the avant-garde writers and artists, pinching Mona Lisa was viewed with irreverent humor. Inspired by the theft, Max Jacob, an entertaining mystic, misogynist, poet, and painter, composed a prose poem about an alarm clock whose inner workings were Mona Lisa's soul. By day, it stopped and started in time with her hapless adventures and the erratic progress of the investigation.

The excitement over the Thief's confession drifted slowly south toward Céret. Since Picasso sent a rushed but carefree postcard to Apollinaire on August 31, the *Paris-Journal* of August 29 probably did not arrive until September 1 at the earliest. When it did, bemused detachment turned to panic. Picasso set out immediately for Paris, leaving Braque to pick up the pieces of their aborted vacation.

3

AS CITIES GO, Paris is compact, spiraling from the center out in concentric circles like a snail shell, with the River Seine flowing through its center. Which came first, the snail shape of the city or Parisians' fondness for escargots, is an open question. Montmartre, one of the highest of the city's districts, is set on a butte, an isolated hill formed by the limestone outcroppings of the ancient town. The streets are steep and narrow, like the stairs in a turret, and at the top, rising like an enormous meringue, is the white eminence of the church of the Sacré-Coeur. Although construction was at a standstill in 1911,* its dominance was already ensured.

Before the scene shifted to the Left Bank, Montmartre was a mecca for struggling artists. Not yet a picturesque tourist attraction, it was a down-at-the-heels quarter where rents were low and nights were lively. Toulouse-Lautrec, Pissarro, Cézanne, van Gogh, Monet, and Renoir had lived and worked there. Now a new generation crowded into the same studios—an eclectic mix of artists, writers, and the occasional anarchist.

Picasso lived at Renoir's old address, 13 Rue Ravignan, a ramshackle wooden tenement carved out of the southwestern slope of the butte. The place was known as *le bateau-lavoir* because it resembled one of the floating river barges where the washerwomen of Paris laundered the linen of the well-to-do, each article acquiring the yellow hue of the Seine. It was in Picasso's single studio room in *le bateau-lavoir* that the "gang" congregated.

Daniel-Henry Kahnweiler, one of the early dealers in the new art, described the squalor: "There was dust on the drawings and rolled-up canvases on the caved-in couch. Beside the stove was a kind of mountain of piled-up lava, which was ashes. . . . It was there that he lived with a very beautiful woman, Fernande, and a huge dog named Frika." Picasso used the stove for heat, an earthenware bowl for a sink, and a rusty frying pan for a chamber pot. He would call those youthful days the happiest years of his life.

"His blue electrician's outfit, his sometimes cruel humor, the strangeness of his art were known throughout Montmartre," Apollinaire wrote. "His studio, crammed with canvases of

---

* The church was completed in 1917.

mystical harlequins and drawings underfoot everywhere that anyone had a right to carry off, was the rendezvous for all the young artists, all the young poets."

In those youthful days, Picasso exuded the intensity of a matador and the swagger of a gangster. He was "short, dark and uneasy in a way that makes you feel uneasy yourself,"* with a thatch of black hair curving down over one enormous dark eye. His eyes were as black and round as eight balls and just as unrevealing.

In the bohemian haunts of Montmartre, Picasso was a charismatic, often contentious presence—jealous and explosive about both his art and his almond-eyed mistress Fernande Olivier. While he painted, Fernande lounged languorously nude and catlike on the mattress that passed for their bed, daubing on expensive perfume, which was her passion, absorbed in the *Katzenjammer Kids*. They would argue over who would read the American comics first.[†] The *Katzenjammer Kids* was their favorite strip.

Fernande was one more artifact amid the chaos of Picasso's studio—Alice B. Toklas described her as "superbly decorative," like "an oriental odalisque." Beside the small, dark Catalan, the statuesque Fernande was a tawny Amazon, auburn-haired and green-eyed. Heads turned when she entered a room. Born Amélie Lang, Fernande had a miserable history of abuse, a loveless childhood, and a failed early marriage. Like everyone in their group, she was inventing herself, leaving behind Amélie Lang and becoming "la belle Fernande," Picasso's first *grand' amour.* He was so wildly jealous that he locked her in his studio, never allowing her to go out without him. He would take the string bag and do the grocery shopping himself.

When the Picassos did venture out, they were in costume.

* Fernande Olivier describes Picasso et al. in her memoir, *Picasso and His Friends.*
[†] The Steins supplied the American funnies.

Fernande in the dramatic hats she adored, looking as if she had wandered off a Toulouse-Lautrec canvas, and Picasso in pegged trousers, brandishing a walking stick like a sword. Apollinaire in his habitual three-piece British suit, and Max Jacob in monocle and a top hat he shared with Picasso, would join them. Their dress was deliberately eccentric. In their person and personality, the friends assumed a studied singularity, a carefully chosen otherness. They were a new breed of artist, and they affected a costume to fit the role.

Fernande's memoir, *Picasso and His Friends,* is the best picture of that band of artistic brothers, the sometimes ignoble few who formed the Picasso gang. They were a fluid group of artists and writers that at any time included Georges Braque, André Derain, Marcel Olin, Maurice Raynal, Ramon Pichot, André Salmon, André Breton, Faik Konica, Blaise Cendrars, and Pierre Reverdy. At the center were Picasso and Fernande; Apollinaire and his lover, the painter Marie Laurencin; and Max Jacob, their court jester performing to hold his place at the round table. He called Fernande's book "the best mirror of the cubist Acropolis."

The years 1905 to 1911 were a magical time of intense creation and extraordinary collaboration. Picasso emerged from his melancholic Blue Period and entered his Rose Period. He took the first steps toward cubism and painted *Les Demoiselles d'Avignon,* the controversial work that, more than any other, revolutionized art and implicated him in *l'Affaire des Statuettes.*

Although Fernande was protective of Picasso until the end of her life, she was an astute mistress-muse, and from the reflections in her looking glass, a modernist creation story emerges. In those happy days, Picasso would sell his art by the armful—a hundred francs (then worth about $20) for a stack of drawings; two thousand francs for thirty canvases. A few dealers—notably Ambroise Vollard, astute and fair, and Clovis Sagot, an unscrupulous ex-clown who sold art out of an old apothecary—were scooping up Picasso's harlequins and saltimbanques for the price of a meal. With youth, brilliance, and a rare bonhomie, money was a luxury, and freeloading was a way of life. "You could owe money for years for your paints and canvases and rent and restaurant and practically everything except coal and luxuries," Picasso remembered.

His fortunes began to change when the Steins discovered him. Leo and Gertrude Stein, a brother-sister act from America, were in Paris then, auditioning for immortality. (In 1911, Alice B. Toklas, small and wary, was a new addition to their ménage.) The Steins' money came from the Omnibus Cable Company of San Francisco. Although not the fortune of a Frick or Carnegie, it was sufficient to bankroll modern art.

Gertrude dressed in a brown corduroy tunic and sandals like a distaff Friar Tuck, and like the outlaws of Sherwood Forest, she and Leo came to the rescue of starving artists with generous patronage and platters of jambon and baguettes. In their studio at 27 Rue de Fleurus, a short stroll from the Luxembourg Gardens, they presided over Saturday soirees that drew an eclectic company of painters, poets, and hangers-on. Although the neighborhood was more shabby than chic, if it were Versailles in the heyday of the Sun King, it could not have attracted a more lustrous, or soon to be lustrous, crowd.

The Steins were as eccentric as the artists they nurtured— the needle-thin and needling pedant Leo, and Gertrude, the monolithic, self-aggrandizing writer. He had pretensions to erudition, she to genius. She recognized it in Picasso and lusted for it, embracing him perhaps in the hope, conscious or subliminal, that his luster would burnish her. In the early years on the Rue de Fleurus, the main draws for the penniless painters and poets were the free food and wine. By 1911, the star attractions were the art that the Steins were collecting, which by then covered the walls floor to ceiling—and the looming talents: Henri

Matisse, a courtly éminence grise at forty-two, and Picasso, the rude contender.

Although everything about *la bande de Picasso,* their art and their attire, was calculated to make a statement, to break from the past and express their freedom and freshness, they created their revolutionary art within certain bourgeois conventions: Saturday evenings at Rue de Fleurus with the Steins; Tuesday-night poetry readings at the Closerie des Lilas; Wednesday-night *daube de boeuf* dinners at Apollinaire's apartment.

4

AS THE BARON'S CONFESSIONS galvanized Paris, Apollinaire grew increasingly alarmed. When Picasso's train pulled into the station, the frantic poet was waiting on the platform. The police had searched his apartment, he said, and Picasso's would be next.

By September 1911, Picasso and Fernande had moved a few blocks from the grungy studio in *le bateau-lavoir* to an airy bourgeois apartment on Boulevard de Clichy. "Fernande began to buy furniture and have a servant and the servant of course made a soufflé," Gertrude Stein wrote. Gertrude's friend Etta Cone found the Picassos "appalling but romantic." Their new apartment was often full of friends, "but on the whole, they were not as happy as they had been."

At the Boulevard de Clichy apartment, Picasso and Apollinaire plotted their next moves. They were not innocents in *l'Affaire des Statuettes.* Buried in the back of a Norman cupboard within easy reach were two figures—a small, powerfully built stone man and woman carved by the ancient Spaniards during the Bronze Age. The bottom of each bore the stamp: PROPERTY OF THE MUSÉE DU LOUVRE.

Painter and poet were expatriates—Picasso was a Spanish citizen, and Apollinaire was a man without a country.* They were afraid of being deported or worse.

Political anarchists were loose in the streets of Europe. In the first decade of the new century, anarchists assassinated three heads of state: Umberto I of Italy in 1900; U.S. president William McKinley the following year; and Russian premier Pyotr Stolypin in 1911. The political and social forces that would lead to the first world war were gathering. In Paris, the Bonnot Gang, armed with repeating rifles and the first get-away cars—more sophisticated equipment than the police had—was agitating the Third Republic. In the Bonnot version of criminal anarchy, the state had no legitimate authority, so every law could be broken. The Bonnot Gang's crimes were rash and violent—murder, bank robberies, and auto, not art, theft. But the police made no distinction between political and cultural anarchists—the "motor bandits" and the émigré artists. Being young, foreign, and male was enough to arouse their suspicion.

Apollinaire and Picasso acted like guilty men, concocting elaborate scenarios to elude the police. First they made plans to flee the country, then abandoned them. Next they hatched a plot to destroy the incriminating evidence. They would pack the stolen goods in an old suitcase and drop it in the Seine at midnight. They pictured themselves as actors in a drama, and they were certain the ending would be tragic.

On the night of September 5, a gang of four—Picasso and

---

* *Le Figaro* wrote in a profile of Apollinaire: "He talks with such precise detail about the landscape and inhabitants of so many countries that nobody knows exactly where he comes from, nor where he has been."

Fernande, Apollinaire and Marie—sat nervously around the dining room table in the Montmartre apartment. Although none of them knew the first thing about cards, like two-bit gangsters and their molls in a B movie, they pretended to play all through the interminable evening.

At the stroke of twelve, painter and poet slunk out to dispose of their contraband. Even following an arrowlike route, the distance from Montmartre to the Seine is probably three miles. They walked the distance because they were afraid to attract attention by lugging a suitcase in a cab or carriage. By the time they reached the river, they were already tired.

Picture the pair—Picasso, small and sullen, and Apollinaire, robust and ribald—skirting the Right Bank in the dead of night, Apollinaire bent at a downward angle and Picasso reaching up because one was so much taller than the other, toting their cheap, scuffed valise, the clothes from the Céret vacation dumped out and replaced with the Louvre stash. At first, they tried to carry the valise between them, but they were too mismatched in size, and so they took turns.

The water was dark, the lamplight picking out the ripples and undulations. They followed the quai, which was some thirty feet below street level. Ivy obscured the stone retaining walls and wrapped around the iron rings where merchant ships once moored. The trees from the street above, mostly chestnuts, leaned toward them, and the trees that bordered the river, mostly planes, reached up. The sky, only a shade lighter than the river, was low and overcast, with no stars to steer by, and blotted out for the most part by the trees and shrubs.

They looked constantly over their shoulders, starting at the slightest sound, fearful of every footstep behind them. Electricity was coming slowly to the City of Lights. In the shadows cast by the uncertain gas flames, they imagined uniformed figures flattened against tree trunks and crouched on the riverbank.

Two hours later, they returned to the studio, trudging up the steep hills of Montmartre, puffing, breathless, exhausted by their paranoia as much as by their aborted mission, still carrying the suitcase and its contents. They had never mustered the courage to act.

Apollinaire spent what remained of the night at the apartment, and in the morning, Picasso brought the incriminating evidence to the *Paris-Journal*.*

5

ALTHOUGH THE NEWSPAPER had promised anonymity, the next day, September 6, *l'Affaire des Statuettes* was again a page-one story:

WHILE AWAITING MONA LISA
THE LOUVRE RECOVERS ITS TREASURE
TWO NEW RESTITUTIONS ARE MADE TO *PARIS-JOURNAL*—THE POSSESSOR OF THE TWO OTHER STOLEN
STATUETTES MENTIONED BY "OUR THIEF" TURNS
THEM IN TO US. THE STONE MAN AND THE STONE
WOMAN ARE IDENTIFIED BY THE ADMINISTRATION.

Paris-Journal *recently restored to the Louvre an antique bust, an example of Iberian art by now famous under the incorrect designation of "Phoenician statuette" employed by the thief, whose curious account of the affair we printed without change.*

Our readers will not have forgotten that in this account he mentioned other statues stolen from the Louvre a few years ago and sold to an art lover. It was not specified whether the sculptures had been bought in good faith or whether the art lover knew their provenance.

---

* Fernande said that Apollinaire turned in the statues. Apollinaire said that Picasso did. The *Paris-Journal* called the person "an amateur painter."

THE TYPEWRITTEN LETTER

Yesterday our mail contained a letter written on a typewriter. This document emanated from the mysterious art lover whose identity neither the cleverness of our fellow newspapermen nor the professional skill of the police has as yet been able to discover.

He asked us, of course, to promise discretion, and offered to come in person in the event that we cared to take the responsibility of returning the stolen statues to the Louvre without involving him. . . .

THE STONE MAN AND THE STONE WOMAN

Our visitor had brought with him the sculptures in question. They correspond to the summary description provided by the thief. One is a man's head with an enormous ear, and the other the head of a woman whose hair is rolled into a kind of twist. The dimensions are approximately those of the statue which we previously restored to the Louvre.

YES, THESE ARE BOTH OBJECTS STOLEN
FROM THE LOUVRE!

At the Louvre, the curator in charge of these antiquities, M. Pottier, declared: "Yes, these are the two objects. They are two fine works from the period corresponding to the end of the Roman Republic."

6

WITHIN TWENTY-FOUR HOURS after the story appeared, Apollinaire was under arrest. On the evening of September 7, two detectives paid a return visit to 37 Rue Gros in Auteuil. They spent an hour combing through the apartment. "Without their help, my correspondence would never have been filed," Apollinaire would joke later. At the time, though, he was too apprehensive to see any humor in his predicament.

The detectives questioned Apollinaire's concierge and neighbors. Was he a sinister character? Had they noticed any suspicious goings-on or deviant behavior? Did he bring home little boys or girls? Anything at all that aroused concern? Later, Apollinaire would say the experience "made me understand the man who said that, if he were accused of stealing the bells of Notre-Dame, he would take to his heels immediately."

There was something of Pierrot, the clown with the tear in his eye, in Apollinaire. He was a paradox—a man with legions of friends, yet alone, making everything up, especially himself, and never quite sure if he had pulled it off. He was the dutiful son who never pleased, the loyal friend who would be betrayed, but he had enormous courage on many levels. As Jorge Luis Borges would write, Apollinaire "was a man of elemental, and therefore, eternal feelings; he was, when the fundaments of earth and sky shook, the poet of ancient courage and ancient honor."

He was born Guillaume Albert Wladimir Alexandre Apollinaire de Kostrowitzky in Rome in the summer of 1880 and nicknamed Kostro. His father was unknown, although Apollinaire liked to hint that a Vatican cardinal might have been in his lineage. His mother was a Polish aristocrat who was expelled from her convent school—the Trinità dei Monti, at the top of the Spanish Steps—and became a *femme galante* in the casino in Monte Carlo. She was "an adventuress, to put it politely," Max Jacob said, and the boy Kostro grew up sharing his mother with a series of "uncles."

In Paris in 1902, he shed Kostro and invented himself as Apollinaire. When asked once for a biographical sketch, he wrote: "I don't know what to say. I have no past, and for that reason I should be happy, like peoples without history. . . . My assets consist of a total lack of money, a knowledge of literature that I believe extensive, a few languages living and dead, and a rather varied experience of life. . . ."

Like so many aspiring poets, Apollinaire scrambled for sustenance and success. He was variously a bank clerk, an art critic, a poet, and a pornographer. As voluble as Picasso was withdrawn, Apollinaire possessed a mixture of nobility and vulgarity, energy and intelligence. For a while, he wrote a column about women authors under the pseudonym Louise Lalanne. (When he tired of the column, he announced that Mademoiselle Lalanne had been abducted by an army officer.) He also edited a series of erotic classics, including the works of the Marquis de Sade, whom he rescued from obscurity. De Sade's definition of art as "the perpetual immoral subversion of the existing order" captured Apollinaire's imagination, imbued his criticism, and came to define the new art.

Apollinaire was a passionate proselytizer, presenting modern art to a world not yet ready to embrace it. He provided the intellectual framework and the rationale for much of the art of the twentieth century. The pure freedom he discovered in the philosophy of the Marquis de Sade was a profound influence, underlying his iconoclasm, his openness to experimentation in art and life, and the imagination he brought to the creation of new canons. In his book *Les peintres cubistes,* Apollinaire expounded on the theory and psychology of cubism. He gave a name and a conceptual context to orphism, and he coined the word "surrealism." Although he was roundly mocked as an obtuse critic and huckster by those he bolstered, he gave legitimacy and attention to Picasso and to many other painters, writers, and musicians.

"Guillaume was extraordinarily brilliant," Gertrude Stein wrote, "and no matter what subject was started, if he knew anything about it or not, he quickly saw the whole meaning of the thing and elaborated it by his wit and fancy carrying it further than anybody knowing anything about it could have done, and oddly enough generally correctly."

She rather grandly described him as having the head of a Roman emperor. In reality, it more closely resembled a potato. The dominant feature was a perfect Pythagorean triangle of a nose, closely abutted by small, birdlike eyes and eyebrows like recumbent commas. For someone who discoursed continuously and with such consequence, it is surprising that his mouth was his most meager feature, the lips like slivers of pimento stuck on a large, doughy face.*

He was his own singular creation, a large man physically, with large appetites for life, art, and friendship. He dressed in English wool regardless of the season, because to someone always trying to overcome his bastard birth and reprobate mother, the British epitomized respectability. He never ventured out without a pipe clenched in his mouth and a hat, which always appeared too small, perched precariously on his large head.

Where Picasso was cocky, Apollinaire was exuberant. Striding across Paris from end to end, writing poetry as he walked, he composed his own autobiography. It was a work of fiction he could live by, a story that would make him legitimate and match his enormous enthusiasms. As Kostro, he had grown up always thinking on his feet, embroidering stories to get by, one step ahead of the law—dodging creditors and absconding from hotels in the dead of night. On September 7, the law caught up with him.

---

* As described by Fernande Olivier in *Picasso and His Friends.*

7

THE ARREST OF Guillaume Apollinaire was a startling development in a startling crime. The "pope of cubism"* was transported in handcuffs to the Palais de Justice, where he was arraigned before Magistrate Drioux. The proceedings lasted well into the night. Apollinaire was told that anonymous sources had linked him to *l'Affaire des Statuettes*—specifically, that he had been in contact with the thief who signed himself Baron d'Ormesan and that he had received the stolen sculptures recently returned to the *Paris-Journal*. If he did not identify the baron, he would be charged with harboring a criminal, possession of stolen goods, and thwarting a police investigation. For hours, Apollinaire refused to provide any information. Finally, after prolonged and fruitless questioning, Judge Drioux signed an arrest warrant. Aghast at the prospect of imprisonment, Apollinaire reluctantly complied.

The Louvre Thief, Baron Ignace d'Ormesan, was Honoré Joseph Géry Pieret, a Belgian in his early thirties who had been living in Apollinaire's apartment and working for him as a secretary of sorts. Apollinaire's fictional d'Ormesan describes himself as "an artist . . . and what is more," he says, "I invented my branch of art myself, and am the only one to practice it." By all accounts, the real Géry was matinee-idol handsome, blithely amoral, probably bisexual, and absolutely irresponsible. His father, a prominent lawyer in Brussels, had committed suicide, and his bereaved mother paid her prodigal son to leave home permanently.

Géry was a disarming and polished social parasite, a

---

* Picasso dubbed him.

vagabond in the engaging French tradition of troubadours, living by his wits and his charm, always tempting fate. He spent four years gallivanting in the American West, then returned to Paris. Like Picasso and Apollinaire, Géry loved the circus. They went to the Medrano Circus most weeks. Picasso painted his harlequins and street performers, Apollinaire put them in his poems, and Géry became a circus promoter. When he wasn't galloping around Paris naked except for chaps, a cowboy hat, and a set of sandwich boards, he stole artifacts from the Louvre as a lark. It was a diversion and favorite pastime. As he was leaving Apollinaire's apartment in the mornings, he would say to Marie, "I'm on my way to the Louvre. Anything I can pick up for you?" Incriminating the Picasso gang was another lark.

In Apollinaire's story, Baron d'Ormesan asks, "Which of us has not a crime on his conscience? . . . For my part, I no longer even count them. But I have committed several which have brought me in quite a lot of money. And if I am not a millionaire today, my appetites rather than my scruples are to blame."

D'Ormesan goes on to tell Apollinaire's first-person narrator, "You are the only person in whom I can confide, because I have known you for so long, and know also that you will never betray me."

Once he revealed Géry's identity, Apollinaire expected to be freed. Instead, he was taken to Le Santé prison, where he was stripped, searched, and locked in a cell. The next day, he was grilled again for hours. Apollinaire admitted that on the now infamous date of August 21, he had bought Géry a train ticket to Marseilles, packed up his friend's belongings, and urged him to leave the country. Instead of being safely out of France, Géry had resurfaced five days later and sold his story to the *Paris-Journal.*

The circumstantial evidence against Apollinaire was damning. Although Géry was a restless rogue never long in one place, Apollinaire always put him up during his various sojourns in Paris and often found him work. He knew that Géry had been in possession of stolen art that originated in the Louvre, yet he had sheltered him, and more damaging, he had aided and abetted his friend's aborted getaway. Mona Lisa and Baron d'Ormesan disappeared on the same day—she from the Louvre, he from Apollinaire's apartment.

Prefect Lépine was confident he had apprehended a ringleader in the international gang of art thieves he had been hunting. All the pieces—target, motive, and opportunity—implicated Apollinaire in Mona Lisa's abduction. It only remained for the poet-provocateur to identify his accomplices. Lépine wanted the names of Géry's other "colleagues"—particularly the painter who had bought the stolen statues. When Apollinaire did not comply, Lépine warned that, unless he cooperated and named the painter, everyone close to him—his mother, Marie, and his brother—would be brought in for questioning and their homes searched. Eventually, Apollinaire gave his interrogators the name they wanted. Even then he tried to protect his friend, insisting Picasso had been "taken advantage of" and never knew the antiquities came from the Louvre.

Picasso and Fernande had been waiting anxiously for word from Apollinaire. "Hearing nothing from our friend, we were worried," she recounted, "but we didn't dare go and see him." Apollinaire had been detained for more than thirty-six hours before news of his arrest broke in *Le Matin.* Over a picture of the poet in handcuffs, the headline of September 9 read:

JUDGE DRIOUX ARRESTS AN ART CRITIC,
M. GUILLAUME APOLLINAIRE, IN CONNECTION
WITH THE EGYPTIAN STATUETTES STOLEN
FROM THE LOUVRE

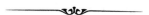
It was not without emotion and surprise that Paris learned last night of the arrest made by the Sûreté in connection with the recent restitution of Phoenician statuettes stolen from the Louvre in 1907.

The mere name of the person arrested is enough to account for this reaction. He is M. Guillaume Kostrowsky [sic], known in literature and art as Guillaume Apollinaire . . . author of a book entitled L'Hérésiarque et cie, *which was a candidate for the last Prix Goncourt.*

Such is the man who was arrested the night before last on the order of M. Drioux, on the charge of "harboring a criminal." What exactly are the charges against him? Both the public prosecutor and the police are making a considerable mystery of the affair.

"Without endangering progress already made," Le Matin was informed, "we can say nothing except that we are on the trail of a gang of international thieves who came to France for the purpose of despoiling our museums."

Apollinaire was one of the most public and popular members of the artistic community of Paris, and his arrest caused such a sensation that Magistrate Drioux was forced to issue a formal statement defending the action. The investigation had "collected evidence tending to show that Guillaume Apollinaire had transgressed against the penal code," the judge wrote. "I will add that his arrest appeared to me to be indispensable to the prosecution of the search made with a view to discovering the Louvre thieves."

The *Paris Herald* reported: "The police believe the theft of the three statuettes to have been the work of a gang of international museum thieves and that this same gang is responsible for the disappearance of *la Gioconda.*" According to Lépine's strained logic, if gang members had possessed the primitive statues stolen from the Louvre, it only remained to uncover where they had stashed the other missing work.

As the story of Apollinaire's arrest broke in the morning paper, the police were rounding up the other ringleader.

8

NINETEEN DAYS AFTER Mona Lisa disappeared, the police paid a visit to Boulevard de Clichy. Picasso, who liked to sleep until noon, was roused at seven a.m. by a persistent knocking at the door. A groggy Fernande, her eyes little more than slits, a gossamer dressing gown wrapped around her extravagant body, opened the door.

The studio presented a scene of eclectic chaos with no concern for color, order, or harmony. In the early light, the chalky silhouette of the Sacré-Coeur gleamed through a high window, looking more like a stage set than a place where sins were confessed and sacrifice offered. Easels and canvases shared studio space with ceremonial African figures, an immense Louis-Philippe couch upholstered in violet velvet with gold buttons, and stolid, ungainly, secondhand furniture that Fernande referred to as Picasso's "Louis XIV style." Suspended randomly and at odd angles on the walls were tattered Aubusson tapestries, primitive masks, battered musical instrument cases, chipped gilt frames, and a lovely, small Corot painting of a woman. Picasso was a compulsive collector.

Six dark, suspicious eyes and six cool baby blues stared from the clutter. The dark eyes belonged to Picasso, now wide awake and trembling with fear; his chattering monkey, Molina; and his white dog, Frika, who looked more like an unshorn sheep than a canine. The baby blues belonged to Picasso's trio of Siamese cats. All eyes were fixed on the intruder.

The detective read a summons from the safety of the doorway, ordering Picasso to appear before the examining magistrate Henri Drioux for questioning. The artist was suspected of dealing in art stolen from the Louvre.

According to Fernande: "Géry, whom Apollinaire had taken to see Picasso, had given the painter two quite beautiful little stone statues, without revealing where he had got them from. He had only said that they should not be exhibited too conspicuously. Picasso was enchanted, and he treasured these gifts." Fernande's account is either naive or disingenuous.

Isolated by the natural barrier of the Pyrenees, the Iberians sculpted a powerful primitive archetype that affected Picasso profoundly. He had visited the Louvre exhibit several times, and he had probably heard the flamboyant Belgian boast of his light-fingered activities. At the very least, Picasso knew the statues he had bought from Géry belonged to the museum. At worst, he may have commissioned their theft, ordering two specific figures from the exhibit, describing exactly which pieces he wanted to use in his new painting—a large, disturbing brothel scene that André Salmon would name *Les Demoiselles d'Avignon*.

If the detective had searched Picasso's studio, he would have found the incriminating evidence. When the police came calling that September morning, *Les Demoiselles d'Avignon* was still in a corner. Picasso had finished the canvas in March 1907 and had shown it to a handful of friends. Even for these avant-garde pioneers, *Les Demoiselles* registered as a deliberate act of scandal. Braque said Picasso was "making us eat cotton waste or swallow gasoline, so we can spit free." Others called it "a shout of insurrection and rage," "a return to barbarism and primitive savagery." Apollinaire was uncharacteristically reticent.

Daniel-Henry Kahnweiler, pretty much alone among the dealers, artists, and friends who saw the painting in Picasso's studio, recognized what he was seeing. He bought all the preliminary drawings and studies and would have bought the canvas, too, but Picasso put it away again. In a 1961 interview, Kahnweiler said: "I could not put a label on it. The picture Picasso had painted seemed to everyone mad or monstrous at the same time. There was something painful and beautiful there, and oppressive but imprisoned."* Reaction was so intense that, four years after finishing it, Picasso had still never exhibited the painting publicly.

Instead of searching the studio, the detective remained pinned at the door by the twelve watchful eyes while Picasso dressed. In an attempt at bravado, the painter chose his favorite red-and-white polka-dot cotton shirt and an elegant silk tie that clashed violently. He was shaking so uncontrollably that Fernande had to button the shirt for him. With his ashen face and vivid outfit, Picasso looked like one of his Rose-Period harlequins.

He was taken by bus from Pigalle to the Palais de Justice. No police vehicle was available. The government would not pay the taxi fare for an alleged criminal, nor was a suspect permitted to spring for a cab. Picasso would never again take the bus that went from Pigalle to Halle aux Vins.

While the police were picking up Picasso, Apollinaire was transported from his jail cell to the Palais de Justice. He was taken in "a kind of cage"† that was very tight quarters for such a large man and very hot. At eleven o'clock, he arrived at the courthouse, where he became the newest in a long line of illustrious and infamous prisoners. The assassin Ravaillac, who stabbed Henri IV; the royal favorite Madame du Barry, mistress of Louis XV; Charlotte Corday and her unrequited lover Adam Lux; Queen Marie Antoinette; and the revolutionaries Danton and Robespierre had all been held there while await-

---

* It should be noted that Kahnweiler was speaking many years later when the painting was widely recognized as a revolutionary work.
† Apollinaire.

ing execution. Apollinaire spent the next four hours in a narrow and stinking holding cell, his face glued to the bars, straining to see who was passing in the corridor.

At three o'clock, a guard led him handcuffed to the courtroom to be arraigned with his accomplice. As the door opened, he was swept up in a surge of reporters and photographers. Some fifty cameras were aimed at him, and the magnesium flashes startled and unnerved him. Later, Apollinaire would say, "I found myself suddenly stared at like a strange beast. . . . I think that I must have laughed and wept at the same time."

Apollinaire and Picasso faced each other across the courtroom like two strangers. Picasso appeared even smaller in that imposing hall of justice. His polka-dot shirt and clashing tie were a gesture of bravado that appeared more pathetic than defiant.

After two days in jail, Apollinaire had a hollow, haunted aspect. He was gray and unshaven, his shirt unbuttoned, the collar torn. His three-piece beige wool suit, much too heavy for the terrible heat, was rumpled and ripped.

The confrontation between the gang leaders had the dimensions of a comic opera gone awry. Seeing the large Apollinaire like "a lamentable scarecrow, gaunt and insubstantial," affected Picasso. He would tell Fernande that he "became completely desperate. His heart failed him even more than it had in the morning when he was unable to dress himself, he was shivering so violently."

Painter and poet were so nervous that in their confusion and desperation to assert their own innocence, truth and friendship were forgotten. They contradicted themselves and each other, each accusing the other of bringing the stolen statues to the newspaper. Both men wept and begged for forgiveness and freedom.

Apollinaire, after being grilled for hours like a criminal, had confessed to everything: harboring Géry, possessing stolen

goods, signing a manifesto that called for burning down the
Louvre. He had implicated and identified Géry and Picasso in
the theft of the Iberian figures. Now Judge Drioux fixed on the
painter. Glaring at Picasso through his pince-nez, he rasped
out questions in his gravel voice. Picasso's tough-guy pose
evaporated like color under turpentine. In his fear, he pleaded
absolute ignorance. He swore that he knew nothing whatever
about *l'Affaire des Statuettes*. He did not know the primitive
Iberian heads were stolen goods, and he did not know Apollinaire. Like Simon Peter when asked, "Do you know this
man?," Picasso replied, "I have never seen him before."

9

EXACTLY WHAT TRANSPIRED in that Paris courtroom
before Judge Henri Drioux depends on who is telling the story.
Apollinaire would recall sometime later: "I thought I was lost,
but the investigating magistrate saw that I had done nothing, and was simply being victimized by police because I had
refused to betray the fugitive to them, and he authorized me to
question the witness; and using the maieutics dear to Socrates,
I quickly forced X to admit that everything I had said was
true." "X," of course, was Picasso, and "maieutics" was a word
only Apollinaire could wield.

Fernande gave a different version, minus both Socrates's
method of eliciting the truth through clever questioning
and Apollinaire's wordplay. Her account was gentler and, as
always, protective of Picasso:

He, too, could only say what the magistrate wanted him to
say. In any case, Guillaume had sworn to so many things, true
and false, that he had hopelessly compromised his friend—he

was in such distress he would have compromised anyone. . . . It has been said that Picasso betrayed his friend and
pretended he didn't know him. That is completely untrue.
He certainly did not desert him, and in fact, his friendship for
Apollinaire seemed to be even stronger afterward.

At the end of the arraignment, Picasso, who had bought
the stolen goods, was released on his own recognizance and
warned not to leave Paris. For weeks afterward, he lived fur-
tively. By nature brooding, he became paranoid, worried that
he would be arrested again. He ventured out only at night, and
then only in a taxi. He was convinced he was being shadowed
and would switch cabs to shake his tail. He slept fitfully,
always listening for another knock at his door.

Apollinaire was returned to the Santé prison, still suspected
of belonging to a gang of international art thieves. Géry, not
without remorse—although it was late in coming—dashed off
a wry note from Frankfurt to the *Paris-Journal* to exonerate
his friend.

*It is deeply regrettable, it is indeed sad, that a kindly, hon-
est, and scrupulous man like M. Guillaume Apollinaire
should be made to suffer for a single moment because of the
personal affairs of someone who was for him only a literary
"subject."*

—*Baron Ignace d'Ormesan.*

With nothing to substantiate the gang of international
thieves except Géry's fanciful fabrication, Apollinaire was
released provisionally on September 13 after a final interrogation, but all charges were not dismissed until January 1912.
Apollinaire's last appearance before Magistrate Drioux was
very different from the previous ones. He knew his bad dream
was ending, and with his wits and wit restored, he parried with
the judge.

The *Paris-Journal* ran the complete transcript:

THE THEFTS IN THE LOUVRE
RELEASE OF M. G. APOLLINAIRE
THE PUBLIC PROSECUTOR REALIZES THAT THE
CHARGES MADE AGAINST THE AUTHOR OF
"L' HÉRÉSIARQUE ET CIE" ARE WITHOUT BASIS.

It was 3 o'clock when Apollinaire, pushing through the crowd of reporters, photographers and friends from the worlds of journalism, letters and the arts, come to bring him the comfort of their sympathy, entered the magistrate's office. A policeman accompanied him. Apollinaire—we deplore this inadmissible harshness on the part of the prison authorities—was handcuffed. [This is] the individual described by the Sûreté as "chief of an international gang come to France to despoil our museums." Even in the Sûreté they write novels—very bad ones! . . .

The magistrate, fingering the meager dossier so laboriously compiled, first questioned him about the origin of his acquaintance with the famous "Baron d'Ormesan."

"You admit that even though you knew it was stolen, you kept that third statue, stolen in 1911, in your house from June 14th to August 21st?" [Géry had stolen from the Louvre three times, twice in 1907 taking the statues that Picasso had bought, and a third time in 1911.]

"Certainly. It was in Géry's suitcase. I kept everything— the man, the suitcase and the statue in the suitcase. I assure you that I wasn't very happy about it, but I did not think that I was committing a serious crime."

"Such a degree of indulgence surprises me," said M. Drioux, who had been following M. Apollinaire with interest.

"Here is part of my reason," said M. Apollinaire, "Géry is a little bit my creation. He is very queer, very strange, and after studying him I made him the hero of one of the last short stories in my L'Hérésiarque et cie. So it would have been a kind of literary ingratitude to let him starve."

"You bought, very recently, it has been alleged, a castle in the department of the Drôme?"

"You must be referring to a castle in Spain. I have seen many of those evaporate."

"I have a letter here from someone who says that you borrowed two books from him, and that one of them, La Cité Gauloise, you never returned."

"I imagine his reason for lending them to me was that I might read them. I haven't read them yet. I will return them to him as soon as I can."

The moment he was released, Apollinaire went directly from the courtroom to the offices of the *Paris-Journal* and dashed off his own account of his jail term.

"*Mes Prisons*" by Guillaume Apollinaire ran in the paper the next day. The account began:

As soon as the heavy door of the Santé closed behind me, I had an impression of death. However, it was a bright night, and I could see that the walls of the courtyard in which I found myself were covered with climbing plants. Then I went through a second door, and when that closed, I knew that the zone of vegetation was behind me and I felt that I was now in some place beyond the bounds of the earth, where I would be utterly lost. I was questioned several times and a guard ordered me to take my "kit"; a coarse shirt, a towel, a pair of sheets, and a woolen blanket; and then I was taken through interminable corridors to my cell, No. 15, Section 11. There I had to strip naked in the corridor and was searched. I was then locked up. I slept very little because of the electric light that is kept on all night in the cells. Everybody knows what prison life is like: a purgatory of boredom, where you are alone and yet constantly spied on.

Later, Apollinaire would call it "strange, incredible, tragic, and amusing all at once" that he was the only person arrested in France for the theft of Mona Lisa.

10

L'AFFAIRE DES STATUETTES may have started as a practical joke instigated by the arts editor for the *Paris-Journal* with Géry's feckless collusion. André Salmon had lived in *le bateau-lavoir.* He was a friend of Apollinaire and Géry, and one of *la bande de Picasso.* Like all the actors in the tragicomedy that played to sold-out audiences in the newspapers and court-rooms of Paris, Salmon was impudent and ambitious.

A slender man in every way—face, physique, and talent—with an acerbic charm, he was a lesser star to the twin suns of Apollinaire and Picasso. Perhaps that tempted him to exploit Géry's chronic quest for easy money. When the opportunity presented itself, Salmon may have devised a humorous ruse that got out of hand. It may have been irresistible to a clever mind like his—a prank, perhaps embarrassing, though with no malevolent intent—but it became something else, something much larger and damaging that he could not control.

Salmon probably intended the "confessions" to be amusing, and they were, but, as noted before, the Paris police were not celebrated for their sense of humor. If he instigated the hoax, Salmon misjudged the mood of Paris, the magnitude of the Mona Lisa theft, the pressure on the police, and the backlash against the cultural anarchists—excoriated as foreign thieves despoiling the museums of Paris. Above all, he misjudged the depth of shame he would bring on his friends. Salmon never admitted that he had played a role in the affair, and he contin-ued to write articles and books. His greatest success would come years later, in his memoirs of that band of creative broth-ers. In *Souvenir sans fin,* he would conjure again the romance of the Picasso gang that he, more than anyone, may have destroyed.

As for Géry, he turned up the next year in Cairo, where he was arrested and eventually acquitted. In his fiction, Apollinaire wrote of Baron d'Ormesan, "Our numerous encounters . . . had given me occasion to appreciate his singular character, his lack of scruples, his somewhat disorderly erudition, and his agreeable and kindly disposition. . . ." In relaying the news of Géry's arrest, Apollinaire wrote, "The poor fellow was crazy rather than a criminal, the courts must have thought so, too."

With the detention of Apollinaire and Picasso, the theft of Mona Lisa assumed an added dimension—a clash of the twentieth-century contender with the Renaissance master. Leonardo's Mona Lisa was a climactic performance of the Renaissance. Picasso's *Les Demoiselles d'Avignon* was the opening act of modern art.

Mona Lisa personified what the Picasso gang was rebelling against, and in *Les Demoiselles d'Avignon*, Picasso painted her antithesis. He was becoming increasingly alienated from the empirical world that Leonardo had drawn from. He destroyed the perspective that Leonardo had mastered, and he obliterated the human face that Leonardo had perfected. The eternal *Gioconda* that could never be surpassed draws us in, holding us entranced. Picasso's whores "stare us down."*

Les Demoiselles d'Avignon has been called "the most worked-on picture in the history of art," and in its initial stage, all the figures had Iberian features. Under the spell of the ancient sculptures from his native Spain, Picasso painted

* John Golding: *Les Demoiselles d'Avignon and the Exhibit of 1988.*

feverishly, creating the huge brothel scene. Sometime later he would say that the asymmetrical faces of the central figures with their angular planes were copied directly from the stolen art. The dominant features were the Iberian eyes, much larger than in life, bulging under "lids like the rim of a cup,"* and the ears, equally oversize and disproportionate, curling like scrolls.

Years later, when it was safe to do so, Picasso admitted that he had used the stolen figures, but even then he blamed Apollinaire for their theft:

> *Les Demoiselles d'Avignon* was the first picture to bear the mark of cubism; it is true. You will recall the affair in which I was involved when Apollinaire stole some statuettes from the Louvre? They were Iberian statuettes. . . . Well, if you look at the ears of *Les Demoiselles d'Avignon,* you will recognize the ears of those pieces of sculpture! . . . From this point of view it is true that cubism is Spanish in origin and that it was I who invented cubism.

After their courtroom encounter, the appearance of friendship between Picasso and Apollinaire continued, but its soul was lost, its heart bled dry. Fernande pinpointed the fatal flaw at the core of *la bande de Picasso:*

> There was hardly anyone in our group who would rush to defend someone who wasn't there. In fact, although they all seemed to be united by strong affection, the minute someone left, the others would start running him down. There can never have been an artistic circle where mockery, spite and deliberately wounding words were more prevalent. There was often a common spirit about art and ideas, but rarely any common affection or generosity, and many of the protestations of admiration or friendship were almost wholly insincere. The worst offenders were Picasso and Max Jacob,

* Ibid.

who could never resist an opportunity for a witticism, which could often be malicious—even at the expense of their greatest friends. Max pretty much spared Picasso—there seemed to be no limits either to his admiration or to his deeply affectionate friendship—but he did not feel the same way about the others. Yet in spite of all this, it was an extremely tight-knit little clique that was hard for newcomers to penetrate.

Mona Lisa's theft and Apollinaire's arrest marked the end of a friendship, the end of Fernande and Picasso, the end of Marie and Apollinaire, the end of the rare bonhomie that produced one of the most exuberant, enchanted, creative collaborations in art history. If, as many have said, Apollinaire's greatest talents were for poetry and for friendship, then in the latter, he was badly served. If he thought he had finally found a firm foundation in the poets and artists whose future he championed and shaped, he was disillusioned. His friends divided. While some demanded his release, many others turned away. The closest to him, Picasso and Marie Laurencin, denied him.

A languid gamin with a complexion the color of antique lace, Marie affected an air of naïveté. Apollinaire described her as having "the somber and childlike face of those destined to make men suffer."* Picasso had introduced them, and Marie, who went to art school with Braque, brought him into their gang, but she was an observer, never a full participant. Myopic and neurotic, she peered at people and paintings through a lorgnette and seemed to approach life obliquely, in this world but not of it. Apollinaire was smitten. Marie's feelings seemed more complex.

She remained silent through his ordeal, refusing to visit him in jail or even to write, and she shunned him when he was released.

Some time after, in a version of his poem *Zone,* Apollinaire

* *Poet Assassinated.*

would write that, like Jesus on the cross, he had lived in Auteuil between two thieves. The good thief was a criminal, and the bad thief was a woman. And because he lived between these two thieves, he was arrested one day for receiving stolen goods.

Apollinaire's sudden notoriety appalled Marie. He had appeared disheveled and handcuffed in newspapers all over the world. The work that he had done to survive, translating and writing erotica, was used to denounce and demean him. The Paris newspapers were highly politicized, and in the conservative press, he was pilloried as a pornographer, sexual predator, reprobate, and rabble-rouser.

Honor was not a grand, empty sentiment to Apollinaire. He had been humiliated publicly, and his loyalty to France questioned. Less than two years later, when war was declared, he enlisted in the French army, joining the Thirty-eighth Artillery. "I so love art that I have joined the artillery," he joked.

Apollinaire wrote his most beautiful poetry in the army.

On the 31st day of August in the year 1914
I left Deauville shortly before midnight
in Rouveyre's little car

Including his chauffeur there were three of us

We said goodbye to a whole epoch
Furious giants were looming over Europe
The eagles were leaving their eyries expecting the sun
Voracious fishes were swimming up from the abysses
Nations were rushing together to know each other through
    and through
The dead were trembling with fear in their dark dwellings

In 1916, on the front line in Champagne, he was injured in the head by shrapnel. He never recovered fully from the physical or the psychological wound. André Billy, a writer and close friend, said:

> Apollinaire's stay in prison left him for a long time with a feeling of terror, and we did our best as friends to help him get over it. He had become a public figure, but he had reached that position via the door that bears the inscription, "All hope abandon, ye who enter here." He was marked for life, and even the war, his courage, and his wound would never succeed in silencing certain persons who, out of ignorance, envy, stupidity, or self-interest, banded against him and continually attacked him as an artist and as a man. He was harassed by slanders to the end of his days, but was too proud to complain.

Apollinaire died on November 9, 1918, two days before the armistice of World War I. He was thirty-eight. Outside his window, jubilant Parisians danced in the street, cheering the end of war and the end of Guillaume. It was a final irony. The Guillaume whose downfall the French were cheering was the German kaiser Wilhelm (Guillaume) II who had abdicated that day.

In an eerie coda to the Apollinaire-Picasso-Géry saga, on the day Apollinaire died, a mutual friend received a note from Géry who claimed to be serving on the Western Front as an officer in the Belgian army. A raven had flown in his open window, and Géry wrote, "I felt I was getting a message from Guillaume Apollinaire. I am very worried about him and beg you to tell me whether he is still alive."*

For years, Picasso never spoke of Apollinaire and the Mona Lisa arrest. He continued becoming Picasso, the most extraor-

---

* John Richardson tells the story in the third volume of his masterly biography of Picasso, *The Triumphant Years, 1917–1932*.

dinary, the wealthiest, and ironically, the most stolen artist of the twentieth century. Perhaps he saw the old gang as youthful folly or embarrassing history. He would sue unsuccessfully to prevent Fernande from publishing her memoir, and he would abandon Max Jacob. In their *bateau-lavoir* years, Max had converted to Catholicism after experiencing two apparitions of the Virgin Mary, his second one in the aisle of a movie theater. Picasso was his godfather. But in the end, neither Max's adopted religion nor his illustrious sponsor saved him. When France fell to the Nazis in World War II, he was arrested by the Gestapo and interned in Drancy. Although mutual friends pleaded, Picasso failed to petition for his release. Max Jacob—Jew, homosexual, poet, artist, most loyal friend, and yearning spirit—died on March 5, 1944, awaiting deportation to a concentration camp in Germany.

On June 20, 1959, almost fifty years after *l'Affaire des Statuettes,* Picasso made a confession of sorts. He spoke to Gilbert Prouteau, a film director who had made a documentary about Apollinaire.*

"I know you," Picasso said when he met Prouteau. *"You are the one who taught me that there is such a thing as remorse, when I saw your film on Apollinaire last year. During the hour I spent watching it, I was thirty years old again. And I think I shed a tear or two."*

"Memories, Maître?" the director asked.

"Yes, but not the kind you are thinking. I can admit it now. I did not behave very well with 'Apo' on one occasion. It was after the affair of the theft of the Mona Lisa. Guillaume had returned the picture in care of a newspaper, but despite that precaution, our little group was being watched rather carefully. . . . We were at the age of the gratuitous act. Such childishness amused us, and the idea of owning a

* The interview was published in the *Paris Presse.*

series of little statues for a few days delighted me. It wasn't robbery, just a good joke. No sooner said than done. But this time the police were ready. I took fright and wanted to throw the package into the Seine. 'Apo' was against it.

" 'They don't belong to us,' he said.

"And he got himself arrested. Naturally, they confronted us. I can see him there now, with his handcuffs and his look of a big, placid boy. He smiled at me as I came in, but I made no sign.

"When the judge asked me: 'Do you know this gentleman?' I was suddenly terribly frightened, and without knowing what I was saying, I answered: 'I have never seen this man.'

"I saw Guillaume's expression change. The blood ebbed from his face. I am still ashamed."

It is a strange confession. In his earlier remarks, Picasso blamed Apollinaire for stealing the Iberian statues from the Louvre exhibit. In this interview, while expressing remorse, in an offhand way he accuses Apollinaire of stealing Mona Lisa. Perhaps Picasso's memory was playing games with him, perhaps he meant to say statue not picture, or perhaps he was still protecting himself.

I I

THE APOLLINAIRE-PICASSO SPECTACLE was a diversion—intriguing, all-absorbing, but ultimately, a fanciful invention, a case of overzealous police work born of frustration and fervid imagination. Although he grudgingly allowed that the Picasso gang leaders were more *enfants terribles* than clever criminals, Prefect Lépine continued to believe an international ring of thieves was behind Mona Lisa's disappearance. The robbery had been too slick to be the work of a lovesick psychotic, a common crook, or any gang of amateurs, and beyond the newspaper headlines, there was no concrete evidence pointing to an American millionaire-collector.

The new director of the Louvre acted quickly to fill the security chasm. He hired more guards, brought in attack dogs, and established new rules. Effective immediately, visiting hours were curtailed to allow for closer supervision. Written permission was required before a work of art could be touched. Several exits were sealed permanently, and the other doors were closely monitored.

Leonardos of one kind or another were making news. In the ongoing arms race in Europe, Italy launched its third dreadnought, the *Leonardo da Vinci,* and one of the best three-year-old thoroughbreds in Europe was named Leonardo. But there was no Mona Lisa. At the traditional Mardi Gras parade in Paris, a huge float showed her taking off in an airplane from the roof of the Louvre.

As the investigation stumbled on, Mona Lisa became the phantom of the Louvre. Her presence had bewitched. Now her absence haunted. When Apollinaire was released from jail, Mona Lisa had been missing for twenty-three days, and each day the public waited to learn if the woman with the shady past had come to a tragic end. Wrapped in the mystery of her baffling disappearance was the enigma of Mona Lisa herself.

THE MYSTERY WOMAN

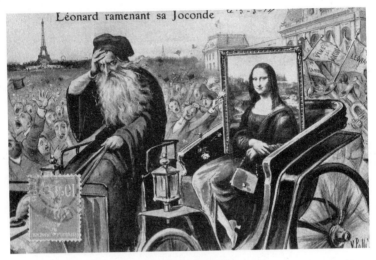

LEONARDO DRIVING MONA LISA

Dating from the time of the theft, this amusing postcard of
Leonardo driving Mona Lisa reflects the popular belief that the
creator had fallen in love with his creation.

(Courtesy of Musée de la Carte Postale, Antibes, France)

I

LEONARDO WROTE THAT a woman should be painted in a demure position, her head lowered and inclined to one side, her eyes cast down modestly so that her gaze never meets the viewer. Then he painted Mona Lisa.

Like a Prometheus, he seemed to breathe life into panel and pigment. While the criminal act was shocking, it seemed almost inevitable. Mona Lisa's presence is so real, her gaze so personal, that no frames could contain her indefinitely. She is too much a woman, too sensual, too vibrant, and it seemed only a matter of time, albeit 109 years, before she moved on.

Who was Mona Lisa, and what was in Leonardo's mind when he painted her? Was she an actual woman who sat for her portrait or a fiction of the painter's imagination? We know from his pupil and secretary Francesco Melzi that Leonardo never threw away a drawing or a page of writing, and he filled thousands of pages with sketches and notes. Yet there is no trace of Mona Lisa in his notebooks—no preliminary studies of her, not a mention, not a jotting. No contracts or bills in the records of the period mention a commission.

Like most Renaissance works, the painting is unsigned, undated, and untitled, and what historical details we have are contradictory. Leonardo, who relished puns and puzzles, left no clue to her identity except her smile. Art historians have been trying to read her body language for centuries. Without props to explain her, she becomes her own narrative, a psychological study as much as an oil painting.

In 1550 the Florentine artist and author Giorgio Vasari christened the painting "Monna Lisa," which in English translation became Mona Lisa. It may be the most famous misspelling in history. Vasari is the richest but not always the most reliable contemporary source on the Renaissance art world. In his book *Lives of the Painters, Sculptors, and Architects,* he identified the sitter as Lisa del Giocondo, the wife of a wealthy silk merchant in Florence.

According to Vasari, Mona Lisa's story began in the wine country of Tuscany, the year after the young Leonardo da Vinci received his first commission. In 1478 the Signoria, the governing authority of Florence, advanced the twenty-six-year-old artist twenty-five gold florins to paint an altarpiece for the Chapel of San Bernardo in Palazzo Vecchio. Leonardo never delivered the work, establishing a precedent that would dog his reputation, but the following year, a successful delivery was made that in retrospect was momentous.

On the fifteenth of June 1479, in the vineyards of Chianti, purple grapes fattening on the vine, in a picturesque farmhouse that is now a picturesque tourist inn called Vignamaggio, a daughter was born to Antonmaria di Noldo Gherardini and his third wife. Since the first two Signore Gherardinis had died in childbirth, the successful delivery of a healthy child was a cause for rejoicing. Antonmaria, a farmer of modest means, named the baby Lisa. Even in Chianti-soaked moments, he could never have dreamed that a young painter from a neighboring town would make her immortal.

Born on April 15, 1452, near the village of Vinci, Leonardo was the product of a romp in the hay between Piero da Vinci and a peasant girl on his father's estate. Like all of Chianti, Vinci belonged to the city-state of Florence, ruled by the Medici, a banking family that had become a political dynasty.

Eventually, Ser Piero would settle down in Florence and become a prominent notary, roughly equivalent to an attorney today.

The Ten Commandments notwithstanding, contemporary society attached no stigma to illegitimacy. Among the eminent bastards of the age were princes, cardinals, and at least one pope, the Medici Clement VII. Raised in his father's house, Leonardo grew up to be a Renaissance Adonis, tall and broad-shouldered with a lithe, athletic build. According to an anonymous contemporary biographer known as Anonimo Gaddiano,* he had "a beautiful head of hair, curled and carefully combed in golden ringlets that fell to the middle of his chest." "At a time when long mantles were fashionable," he dressed in knee-length rose-colored velvet tunics that showed off his legs. Gifted in every art and possessed of an eclectic, endlessly curious mind, Leonardo did not blend into the landscape.

Renaissance artists were traveling salesmen, brushes and chisels for hire, traveling from city-state to city-state, competing for commissions. No longer bound to a specific guild as they had been in the Middle Ages, artists were independent contractors. Packing their pigments and saddling their horses, they shuttled from prince to prelate. Painting on canvas was just coming into vogue. (Michelangelo dismissed it as a pastime for dilettantes.) Most paintings were murals, and artists went wherever the work was, moving from town to town, from Florence to Mantua, Perugia to Milan, Urbino to Rome, and beyond. The best were sought after and liberally paid. Their reputation was spread by envoys, ambassadors, and warring princes who came to Italy for conquest and found culture and a new art.

After apprenticing in the workshop of the Florentine sculptor and painter Andrea del Verrocchio, Leonardo left the

* "Joyfully Anonymous."

humanist cradle of Florence for the sinister court of Ludovico Sforza, the prince of Milan who was known as *il Moro*—the Moor—because of his dark mien and brooding disposition.

Leonardo, whose title was *ingeniarius ducalis*—the duke's inventor—thrived at the Sforza court. Far from being the rebel of myth, he was a skilled courtier and something of a dandy, as adept at the art of flattery as he was at everything else. According to Paolo Giovio, his biographer and a personal acquaintance, he was "the arbiter of all questions relating to beauty and elegance, especially in pageantry." He was "the delight of the entire court . . . by nature very courteous, cultivated and generous, and his face was extraordinarily beautiful."

Leonardo's concern was the knowable, not the inexorable. Wrestling with the eternal questions was left to his rival Michelangelo, twenty-two years younger. An 1861 commentary on the Renaissance masters described Michelangelo as an anguished modern titan and Leonardo as the cool observer without serious vices or great virtues who "never penetrated so far as the moral world . . . never knew the storms of sentiment and the heart where lightning is divine light, and thunder sacred words."*

"To me," Leonardo wrote, "it seems that those sciences are vain and full of error which are not born of experience, mother of all certainty, first-hand experience which in its origins, or means, or end has passed through one of the five senses. And if we doubt the certainty of everything which passes through the senses, how much more ought we to doubt things contrary to the senses—*ribelli ad essi sensi*—such as the existence of God or of the soul or similar things over which there is always dispute and contention."

What today we see as the intellectual flights of a genius who was centuries ahead of his time are often the efforts of a dedi-

* Charles Clement.

cated empiricist to understand what he had observed. From a close observation of nature and an exhaustive recording of what he saw, Leonardo analyzed how things worked, then he used that knowledge to create "visual fictions." Painting is poetry that is seen, Leonardo said, and like the poet, the painter must compose "fictions that express great things." Leonardo applied art to science and science to art. His studies of the muscles that move to form a smile, the dilation of the pupils in response to light, and the flow of water are evidenced in Mona Lisa.

While Leonardo ventured off to Milan, Lisa Gherardini stayed close to home. She must have been pretty and precocious, because just before her sixteenth birthday, she vaulted up the social ladder, marrying Francesco del Giocondo, a thirty-five-year-old widower with an infant son. To seal the marriage contract, her father gave Francesco a farm that he owned on a ridge of hills in Poggio between Florence and Siena, and one hundred seventy gold florins.

Francesco was quite a catch, especially for a girl with such a modest dowry. (Francesco's four sisters each had a dowry of one thousand florins.) His first wife, Camilla Rucellai, had belonged to a leading Florentine family, and Francesco was described in the marriage contract as *civis et mercator,* a citizen and merchant. By 1503, when Lisa probably met Leonardo for the first time, the Giocondos were living in a fashionable new house on Via della Stufa with their growing family—Bartolomeo, Piero, and the baby Andrea. A daughter Camilla, named for Bartolomeo's mother, the first Signora Giocondo, had died four years before.

Leonardo's circumstances were not as easy. In 1499 the French had wrested Milan from the Sforzas. Leonardo remained to complete his fresco of the Last Supper, then he returned to Florence. At the Sforza court, he had been the star attraction for almost twenty years. When he returned to Florence, he faced both professional contenders and political confusion.

Leonardo had left the city as a young man in the glory days of Lorenzo the Magnificent, when the Renaissance was in full flower. Now he was almost fifty. Lorenzo was dead, his disappointing sons had been run out of town, and the Renaissance was migrating south. By 1503, artists were flocking to Rome to work for the formidable new pope and patron, Julius II, and younger artists were challenging Leonardo's preeminence. Michelangelo Buonarroti, just turning thirty, was completing a colossal *David,* and the even younger Raphael Sanzio, a precocious talent, was absorbing the art of his elders, eager to outshine them. No longer the unchallenged master, his finances strained, Leonardo da Vinci was looking for work.

His father, Ser Piero, by then an eminent notary and well connected, probably wrangled a commission for his cash-poor son. Ser Piero had recently settled a financial dispute for a wealthy silk merchant, and sometime during that unsettled decade, Leonardo began a portrait of the merchant's wife, Lisa.

2

ALTHOUGH THE EXACT DATE remains in dispute, Leonardo probably began to paint Mona Lisa in the winter of 1503. He spent that February and March in Florence. Raphael was also in the city, and he must have seen the unfinished work, because he copied Mona Lisa's pose for his own portrait of a Florentine woman, Maddalena Doni, completed in 1504. New evidence confirms the year.

In the 1500s, the art world was fiercely competitive. Artists inspired and learned from one another, borrowing, copying, and sometimes stealing ideas. From the first glimpse on Leonardo's easel, Mona Lisa caused a stir. She was his last-known work, and purely as a technical achievement, she was a revelation. Before Mona Lisa, few portraits went beyond a physical likeness. Most seemed static and impassive, the body cut off, just the head and shoulders depicted. Mona Lisa is painted at eye level and almost life-size, both disconcertingly real and transcendent.

Many artists made detailed studies and drew the outline of their paintings on the canvas or panel before they began to paint. X-rays reveal no underlying drawing and few pentimenti, false starts, or adjustments. Leonardo painted Mona Lisa directly, changing only the placement of the hands and fingers.

She sits on a loggia, or balcony, in a *contrapposto* position, her body angled and her face turned out, creating the arresting impression that she is looking directly at the viewer. Behind her is a low wall, and beyond that, a desolate landscape. Not a leaf, not an animal track to suggest life. Framing her on either side is a partial column that appears cropped. Since the columns are painted over the landscape, Leonardo probably added them toward the end, but what may have been an afterthought became a source of conjecture among art historians. They argued for years that Mona Lisa was originally a larger work with full columns and that the painting was cut down at some point, perhaps to fit a frame. Recent scientific studies using radiography and three-dimensional digitization should end the debate: Leonardo painted only partial columns. The original dimensions of the panel are clear, although the back was planed at some point, reducing the thickness of the original wood.

In the early 1500s, oil painting was a new medium, just beginning to replace tempera, and it involved considerable trial and error. Painters did not know how their methods and materials would stand up over time. If the primer was too thin, the painting would eventually deteriorate. If it was painted on, say, a red ground, the colors would darken.

Leonardo was always experimenting. To paint Mona Lisa, he took a delicate technique often used in watercolors, called *sfumato,* a "vanishing into smoke," and applied it to oils. Using fine silk brushes to eliminate any trace of individual strokes, he applied very thin successive layers of paint and glazes so fine as to be almost evanescent. Leonardo made Mona Lisa a study in chiaroscuro—a painting of light and shadow. Her image is soft and blurred around the edges like a photograph slightly out of focus.

The *contrapposto* position, the hallucinatory background, and the *sfumato* technique were startling innovations in 1503. Vasari called her "revolutionary" and believed that Leonardo had endowed her with extraordinary powers of enchantment.

She is a strange painting—a juxtaposition of extremes. A woman pregnant with possibility and ambiguity is set against a barren world, apocalyptic or post-apocalyptic. Like the woman, the background may be real or imaginary, but the two sides are not aligned. If the figure were removed, like poorly hung wallpaper, the edges would not match.

Adding to the strangeness, the figure and the landscape have distinct perspectives. She is seen vertically at eye level, but the background is an aerial view. Instead of creating a confused or disjointed effect, the double vision is strangely evocative, suggesting almost an optical illusion that enhances the mystique. What is a beautiful young woman doing in such a desolate place? She has a hint of décolletage, a suggestion of spreading hips, the result of childbirth, most likely. Although it is barely discernible with the naked eye, recent digital studies suggest that she is wearing a *guarnella,* a transparent netting that women of the Renaissance wore over their dresses when they were pregnant. Lisa del Giocondo was not pregnant in 1503, but from the outset, Leonardo's intention seemed more than simply fulfilling a routine commission to render a particular likeness.

Financial records suggest that he agreed to paint the silk merchant's wife solely for financial gain. Portraiture may not have appealed to him. He had done only a few others, with significant time spans between them, and he had avoided numerous requests. Isabella d'Este, the Marquise of Mantua and the sister-in-law of his longtime patron Ludovico Sforza, repeatedly asked Leonardo to paint her portrait. She was arguably the most powerful and interesting woman of her time, and not easily denied. Why did Leonardo put off Isabella d'Este but agree to paint a sweet though undistinguished young matron?

Mona Lisa was a departure for him. In his other portraits of privileged women, the subjects are dressed for posterity. Ginevra de' Benci has the curled hair and laced bodice of an upper-class Florentine. *Lady with an Ermine* is clearly identifiable as a mistress of Ludovico Sforza, probably Cecilia Gallerani. The ermine was an emblem of *il Moro,* and the headband and double necklace were fashionable in the Sforza court.

Mona Lisa wears no hint of rank, wealth, or fashion. She would never win the golden apple. Her forehead is too broad, her lips too thin, her figure less than Greek. She is certainly not a fashion plate. Her dress is nondescript, the color and design devoid of style. Leonardo stripped her of all adornments. He allowed her none of the artifice that women since ancient times have employed to enhance their allure. She herself—not her accoutrements—fascinates.

If Mona Lisa is not the most beautiful, fashionable, or glamorous woman, she is the most beguiling. It is the immediacy of the image—caught in a moment, like the frame of a film—that enthralls. She touches without words, offering not a kiss or a caress but the anticipation. She catches us looking at her, and like a woman surprised in the bath, the embarrassment is ours, not hers. If we try to look away, she follows us and will not let go.

Art historians suggest that Mona Lisa evolved over time from an individual to an archetype—with all the attributes of Eve before and after the fall. But the painting suggests the opposite. Consider the dress. It is dull and drab. A border of *vinci,* or knots—a device that recurs like a doodle in the artist's notebooks—delineates the neckline. Otherwise, the dress is as plain as a nun's habit.

Lisa's husband showered her with silk dresses, veils, and jewels. Her wardrobe and jewelry were of sufficient value to be noted in his will. Would a pretty young woman with a wealthy husband and an armoire full of the finest silks—especially one who had not grown up with such luxury, being painted for the first time by a celebrated artist—choose a drab brownish dress to wear and no jewelry? Would any woman?

Lisa's portrait would hang on the wall of her new house for all to admire. She would want to look her most beautiful. She probably spent hours trying on one dress after another before settling on the perfect one, then choosing jewelry to complement it. Leonardo himself dressed elegantly. By his own account, "The painter sits before his work, perfectly at his ease and well-dressed, and moves a very light brush dipped in delicate color; and he adorns himself with whatever clothes he pleases."

Perhaps Lisa's original choice was fuchsia silk and flattering, and the painter insisted she change into her plainest dress. Leonardo da Vinci was a charismatic personality and more than twice her age. Not wanting to offend him, she would have acquiesced with secret reluctance. She was only in her twenties, a young mother, new to the more aristocratic society of the city, newly moved to a fancy house, and perhaps unsure of herself. She may have lacked the confidence, or been too polite, to protest. But her disappointment must have been transparent, because Leonardo went to great lengths to dispel her gloom. He brought in an orchestra of musicians to cheer her, Vasari says, yet the most Mona Lisa could muster was the trace of a smile.

It must have been a galling time for Leonardo. Donato Bramante, his old friend and collaborator from the Milan days, was in Rome building the monumental new Basilica of St. Peter. His young challengers were also being called to the Vatican—Michelangelo to sculpt a massive tomb for Pope Julius and later to paint the Sistine ceiling, Raphael to fresco the rooms of the Papal Palace. While they were in Rome becoming immortal, Leonardo was painting the young Signora del Giocondo. He would not make it a simple portrait.

Mona Lisa may have been a conscious bid for immortality—Leonardo setting out purposefully to conjure from shadow and light a woman who would exert a fatal attraction over men. He believed that he possessed the power. In his notes on painting, he wrote:

> The painter can so subdue the minds of men that they will fall in love with a painting that does not represent a real woman. It happened to me that I made a religious painting which was bought by one who so loved it that he wanted to remove the sacred representation so as to be able to kiss it without suspicion. Finally, his conscience prevailed over his sighs and lust, but he had to remove the picture from his house. . . .

> If the painter wishes to see beauties to fall in love with, it is in his power to bring them forth, and if he wants to see monstrous things that frighten or are foolish or laughable or indeed to be pitied, he is their Lord and God.

Some believe that Leonardo succeeded so well, he seduced himself. Whatever his intention, Mona Lisa is a continuum of desire. History has proved no defense against her, or age, fading grace, or darkening palette.

By pure coincidence, a few days after the theft, the American publisher Thomas Y. Crowell published the English translation of a journal purportedly kept by the painter. The dilapidated manuscript, allegedly discovered in a Renaissance palace in Florence, recounted his romance with his Gioconda.* Petrarch had his Laura, Dante his Beatrice, and, Romantics liked to imagine, da Vinci had his Mona Lisa. Leonardo was cast as Pygmalion and Mona Lisa as his Galatea. After she vanished, a popular postcard pictured Mona Lisa returning to town in a carriage driven by Leonardo.

Today we know from the sophisticated tests conducted at the Louvre that Leonardo painted Mona Lisa's heart at the very center of the composition and made it the most luminous point.

3

MONA LISA TOOK LEONARDO years to achieve, as long as it took Michelangelo to fresco the Sistine ceiling. For each square yard Michelangelo covered, Leonardo painted about an inch. He was legendary for jumping from project to project and completing few of them. As Vasari wrote, "His knowledge of art, indeed, prevented him from finishing many things which he had begun, for he felt that his hand would be unable

---

* This was an old romantic notion, probably instigated by the French historian Jules Michelet, and embraced by the author Julius Verne and the Italian Romantic poet Enrico Panzacchi.

to realize the perfect creations of his imagination, as his mind formed such difficult, subtle and marvelous conceptions that his hands, skilful as they were, could never have expressed them."

But Leonardo painted Mona Lisa intermittently for four years and carried her with him until the end of his life. She must have been with him in 1515 when he returned to Milan and met François I. Whether it was love at first sight or a gradual seduction, the young French king became infatuated with Mona Lisa.

From Paolo Veronese's panoramic *Wedding Feast at Cana*, François I gazes across the Louvre gallery at the beguiling southern temptress who had captured his fancy so many years before. The destinies of the two have converged at surprising, seemingly random points. Through their centuries-long history together, they shared separation, reunion, and a sumptuous bath, and now in the Louvre, not one hundred feet apart, they share the home that François transformed from a gloomy medieval fortress into a Renaissance palace.

In Veronese's crowded tableau, the French king sits at a long wedding table where the A-list of sixteenth-century society has gathered to celebrate the marriage of Eleanor of Austria. François occupies the place of honor on the right hand of the bride; Mary Tudor of England is on her left. Others in attendance are François's rival Emperor Charles V; the Ottoman potentate Suleiman I; and the Italian noblewoman, poet, and cherished friend of Michelangelo, Vittoria Colonna. Wine is flowing, and there is music provided by a singular orchestra of artists. Veronese and his friends have put aside their brushes and taken up assorted instruments. He and Tintoretto are playing the cello. Titian is on the bass, and Jacopo Bassano is playing the flute.

In the fresco, François I appears to be middle-aged, his face and figure thickened but still strong, a man just beyond the prime of life but younger than Leonardo was when prince and painter met for the first time. Leonardo was sixty-three then, and he possessed the aura of mystery that attends genius. François, only twenty-one and new to the throne, was a young Goliath, a strapping seven-foot force of enthusiasm and ambition. What he lacked in looks, he made up for in his exuberant personality.

Like his English contemporary and friend Henry VIII, another young king who lived fast and hard and died spent, François was a true *galant,* a man of immense optimism and appetites. He lusted for beauty in its manifold forms—beautiful art, beautiful architecture, beautiful lovers, beautiful wives. He is famously quoted as saying, "A court without ladies is a springtime without roses." When he joined the club of European monarchs, he was eager to take on the world—to outconquer and outshine the emperor Charles V,* to claim more territory, collect more art, bed more beauties, shoot more boar, and import the best and the brightest talents to France.

François seems like an overgrown boy as he cavorts through history, returning to Italy again and again for art and adventure, conquest and culture. He loved and admired all things Italian. The hunting lodge of Fontainebleau, his favorite palace, had nothing comparable to the large and evocative fresco Leonardo had completed on the refectory wall of the Convent of Santa Maria della Grazie in Milan. New to the throne and new to Renaissance art and artists, François was so affected by *The Last Supper* that he wanted to move the entire

---

* Charles V ruled an empire that made the Caesars look land-poor. At the peak of his power, it was twenty times larger than the Roman empire and comprised the Hapsburg kingdom of Austria; Germany, Luxembourg, and the Netherlands; Naples, Sicily, and Sardinia in Italy; Burgundy and Artois in France; Spain, Mexico, and Peru.

wall to France. When that proved impractical, he offered to import its creator instead.

Born in the Florence of the Medici, the Renaissance had moved to Rome in the extraordinary papacy of Julius II. After the pope's death, François aspired to recenter it in Paris. He brought Italian artists to France, turned the Louvre fortress into a palace, and began to collect the art that would become the nucleus of its collection. His most celebrated coup was persuading Leonardo to emigrate.

According to Vasari, "so great was Leonardo's genius . . . that to whatever difficulties he turned his mind, he solved them with ease," yet by 1515 he had endured more than a dozen uncertain years without a secure patron or a stable sinecure. Although the king offered him generous patronage, royal protection, and a château in the Loire valley near the royal manor house in Amboise, Leonardo vacillated. While he had a restless mind, he had firm roots in the Italian peninsula. He had spent virtually his entire life between Florence and Milan, a distance of fewer than two hundred miles. His imagination roamed, but never at the expense of personal and professional security. After another unsettled year spent mostly in Rome, Leonardo accepted the king's invitation. He moved to France in the summer of 1516.

Leonardo was accustomed to both adoring disciples and the whims and egos of patron-princes, and in France, he found sanctuary. François gave him the charming manor house, Clos-Lucé. The king welcomed so many Italian artists and visitors to his court that Vasari described Fontainebleau as "almost a new Rome." Among those who crossed the Alps were Leonardo's old friend Niccolò Machiavelli; the painter Primaticcio; the architect Sebastiano Serlio; and later, the celebrated fabricator and goldsmith Benvenuto Cellini.

In France, Leonardo was the first among equals. According to Cellini, the king was "extremely taken with his great virtue. . . . He believed there had never been another man born in the world who knew as much as Leonardo."

4

IN OCTOBER 1517, Luigi Cardinal d'Aragona visited France. Wealthy, cultivated, and well connected (his father was the bastard son of the king of Naples, and his cousin was Queen Isabella of Aragon), the cardinal was a quintessential Renaissance prince of the Church, with all that entailed: material riches, intellectual curiosity, a beautiful mistress and daughter, enormous ambition, and an utter absence of scruples. It was rumored that he murdered both his sister, the Duchess of Amalfi, and her husband. The cardinal's European trip combined business and pleasure. He was curious to see the world beyond Italy and eager to gain the support of the rulers of Europe. He had hoped to follow Julius II as pope. Now he was lobbying to be named the king of Naples.

Autumn is beautiful in the Loire valley, and while Cardinal d'Aragona was visiting King François at Fontainebleau, he also stopped in to see Leonardo, who was nearing the end of his work and his life. The cardinal's secretary, Antonio de Beatis, kept an enthusiastic journal of their trip, and he describes the visit in some detail. Leonardo showed them three paintings: a Madonna and child with St. Anne; a young John the Baptist; and a portrait that he called "a certain Florentine lady done from life at the instigation of the late Magnificent Giuliano de' Medici."

Some thirty years later, in his *Lives of the Painters, Sculptors, and Architects*, Giorgio Vasari wrote: "Leonardo undertook to execute, for Francesco del Giocondo, the portrait of

Monna Lisa, his wife." Although he never saw the painting, Vasari rhapsodized over it:

> Whoever wished to see how far closely art could imitate nature was able to comprehend it with ease; for in it were counterfeited all the minutenesses that with subtlety are able to be painted, seeing that the eyes had that luster and watery sheen which are always seen in life, and around them were all those rosy and pearly tints, as well as the lashes, which cannot be represented without the greatest subtlety. The eyebrows, through his having shown the manner in which the hairs spring from the flesh, here more close and here more scanty, and curve according to the pores of the skin, could not be more natural. The nose, with its beautiful nostrils, rosy and tender, appeared to be alive. The mouth, with its opening, and with its ends united by the red of its lips to the flesh-tints of the face, seemed, in truth, to be not colors but flesh. In the pit of the throat, if one gazed upon it intently, could be seen the beating of the pulse. And indeed, it may be said that it was painted in such a manner as to make every valiant craftsman . . . tremble, and lose heart. . . .
>
> Monna Lisa, being very beautiful, he always employed, while he was painting her portrait, persons to play or sing, and jesters, who might make her remain merry, in order to take away that melancholy which painters are often wont to give to the portraits that they paint. And in this work of Leonardo's, there was a smile so pleasing, that it was a thing more divine than human to behold; and it was held to be something marvelous, since the reality was not more alive.

To extol a work with such unrestrained enthusiasm, sight unseen, indicates that Mona Lisa was well known in the art circles of Florence, but Vasari's rhapsody has been raising eyebrows ever since. What eyebrows? Whose eyebrows? Mona Lisa has none. Never have eyebrows, or the singular lack of them, provoked so much discussion and theorizing, or spawned so many academic careers.* The conspicuously missing eyebrows threw Vasari's entire account into doubt.

His description provoked questions that were still being debated in 1911. If Vasari was wrong about her eyebrows, was he also wrong about her identity? Why did Leonardo, standing in front of a painting—presumably Mona Lisa—in France in 1517 describe it as "a portrait of a certain Florentine lady, done from life at the instigation of the late Magnifico Giuliano de' Medici"?

Giuliano de' Medici was one of the sons of Lorenzo the Magnificent, expelled from Florence when the Medici lost power. He had lived in exile in Rome for years. Why would he commission a portrait of a silk merchant's wife? There was no question of an affair between them. Lisa del Giocondo had never left Florence, and Giuliano de' Medici could never return. Did Leonardo paint two Mona Lisas—one for Giuliano de' Medici, never finished because he died in 1516, and one for Francesco del Giocondo, never delivered? Or was he describing a different painting entirely? If Mona Lisa is not Lisa del Giocondo, the silk merchant's wife, who is she?

Da Vinci scholars have scrutinized Vasari's passage and the cardinal's travel log as closely as the Rosetta Stone. To add to the conundrum, when Vasari wrote his account, Mona Lisa was gracing the French king's bathroom, and the earliest royal inventories identified her alternately as "a courtesan in a gauze veil" and "a virtuous Italian lady."

Art historians puzzling over Mona Lisa's identity have suggested many candidates. She is Isabella of Aragon, Beatrice d'Este the Duchess of Milan, one of Giuliano de' Medici's

---

* In 1625 Cassiano dal Pozzo wrote: "Note that his Lady, in other respects beautiful, is almost without eyebrows, which the painter has not recorded, as if she did not have them." When Pozzo was writing, Mona Lisa had been varnished badly at least once, which could have erased her brows. An ongoing digital study suggests that she did have eyebrows once.

many mistresses—probably Pacifica Brandano or Costanza d'Avalos—or she may be his wife, Philippa of Savoy, aunt of François I, which could explain why the king was so eager to own her. Others contend that she is an idealization, a self-portrait of the artist, even a man in drag.

In a valiant effort at reconciliation, one biographer of Leonardo imagined a Romeo-and-Juliet romance between Giuliano de' Medici and Lisa, young lovers at fifteen, cruelly parted when the Medici were routed from Florence. In this scenario, Giuliano, living in exile in Rome, where his brother was pope, asked Leonardo to paint his first love, by then a presumably contented wife and mother.

In spite of the many theories to the contrary, Vasari's identification is the most credible. He had many opportunities to get his facts straight. Lisa del Giocondo née Gherardini was widowed at fifty-nine and died four years later, in 1542. Florence was a small town, the Giocondos were a prominent family, and Vasari's book was a huge best seller.

If he had made an error as egregious as misnaming the subject, someone in the small tight circle of Florentine artists—one of Lisa's sons, for example, or Francesco Melzi, the vigilant keeper of the da Vinci flame, whom Vasari very likely consulted for his history—would have insisted on a correction. That Vasari misidentified the sitter in the first place is unlikely; that he did not correct his mistake in the second edition, published in 1568, is implausible. He fixed several minor errors. (For instance, he had mistakenly referred to Francesco as Lisa's brother.)

Through the years, layers of meaning were applied to Mona Lisa like *sfumato*. The uncertainties surrounding her identity became an ongoing controversy that generated a vast *Gioconda* literature. Misjudgments, scant records, and false assumptions heightened the intrigue. The facts were blurred, the truth obscured.

When Mona Lisa vanished in 1911, her identity was still an open question. Even today, when new research supports Vasari's contention,* da Vinci scholars remain divided. What is indisputable truth to one expert is dubious evidence to another.

5

LEONARDO DIED WITHIN TWO YEARS of the cardinal's visit without in any way resolving the confusion he had caused and raising further questions. He always had several young men in his household as students, assistants, companions, and servants. For many years, Francesco Melzi and Leonardo's adopted "son and heir," the notoriously fickle Salai, had been the closest to him. They were opposites—aristocrat and urchin, prince and prodigal. Giovanni Francesco Melzi was a noble young man, intelligent, talented, and devoted to his master. He came to Leonardo as a student and became his confidant and companion in his old age. Giovanni Giacomo di Pietro Caprotti was ten when Leonardo adopted him. He was Leonardo's bane and joy, an impudent rascal and trouble-maker with the face of a seraph. Leonardo named him Salai— little devil—and indulged him endlessly. Salai did not survive long without Leonardo's protection. He was killed in a street brawl, probably in 1524.

In Leonardo's last will and testament, written days before his death, he bequeathed all his work, both writings and art, to

---

* In January 2008, Reuters News Service reported that German scholars discovered a note in a book belonging to Agostino Vespucci, a city official in Florence. He must have been a punctilious bureaucrat, because he jotted in the margin of his collection of Cicero's letters that Leonardo da Vinci was working on a portrait of Lisa Gherardini del Giocondo, wife of a silk merchant, and he dated his note 1503.

Melzi. Nonetheless, when Salai died, he had twelve paintings in his possession, including "two portraits of women, the second called *la Ioconda.*" According to a contemporary accounting, as late as 1531, Salai's sisters still owned *Ioconda* and six other works. At some point between that date and François I's death in 1547, Mona Lisa returned to France.

The king paid dearly to possess her. Father Pierre Dan, a Jesuit who cataloged the royal art collection in the seventeenth century, noted that François spent the extravagant sum of four thousand gold crowns—the equivalent of nearly twelve tons of pure silver, or about $9.7 million today—for Mona Lisa, the *"premier en estime, comme une merveille de la peinture"*—the most esteemed work in the royal collection, a miracle of painting. But exactly when the purchase was made and from whom are as murky as everything else about her.

Mona Lisa began her new life in Fontainebleau in the Appartement des Bains, the king's luxurious bathroom. Far from being merely or even extravagantly functional, the Appartement des Bains was a six-room suite—an exclusive men's club where François and his guests could indulge, and overindulge, every whim. The rooms included a bathing pool, steam room, gambling room, and lounge, all elaborately frescoed. The king's growing art collection was on display. Since painters were often on hand to immortalize royal favorites in the bath, Mona Lisa was probably copied a number of times.

The Appartment des Bains was not a choice spot for an art collection. Steam and oil paint do not mix well, but it took some fifty years for the royal heirs to realize the hazards in even the most luxurious bathroom. The king's collection was moved upstairs to the newly named Cabinet des Tableaux, later called the Pavillon des Peintures.

In the ensuing decades, Mona Lisa narrowly escaped a swap—the Stuart king Charles I of England offered to trade a Titian and a Holbein for her—and suffered a shellacking.

Perhaps in a misguided effort to repair the effects of her bath-room days, Mona Lisa received a thick coat of lacquer. The Dutch painter Jean de Hoey or his son Claude, keepers of the royal collection in the early 1600s, may have been the guilty parties. The clumsy conservation first dulled, then destroyed, Leonardo's colors. Over time, the varnish cracked, producing a surface web of fine fissures called *craquelure.*

Spared from further ravages of humidity, her luster darkening beneath the heavy varnish, Mona Lisa rested undisturbed and largely unnoticed in the upper floor of Fontainebleau for a further fifty years, until another young king came courting and swept her away. Although a century separated them, the Valois François I and the Bourbon Louis XIV shared a love for all things Italian—humanist thought, Renaissance restraint, and the bewitching Lisa. Louis moved her from Fontainebleau to his new palace in Versailles.

The longest-reigning monarch in European history, Louis XIV was crowned in 1643 at the age of five and sat on the throne for seventy-two years. Like François, he imagined Paris as the center of the world and the Louvre as a magnificent Italianate palace, and like François, he wanted to import the foremost Italian artist. In the seventeenth century, that was the divinely talented, supremely arrogant Gianlorenzo Bernini. The fact that Bernini was the pope's architect, in the throes of an ambitious project to build a square the size of the Colosseum in front of the new St. Peter's Basilica, did not weaken the French king's resolve.

Although he had moved his court and his Mona Lisa to Versailles, Louis wanted to complete the transformation of the Louvre that François had begun. When diplomacy and sweet talk failed to persuade Pope Alexander VII to share Bernini, the Sun King resorted to more militant tactics. With the French spurred and booted to invade Italy, the pope capitulated. In 1655 he agreed to lend his architect to France for three months to build the Louvre. It was not as happy a sojourn as Leonardo's.

From Bernini's first day in Paris, the enterprise was a disaster. He was taking a siesta when the king's minister arrived to greet him, and relations deteriorated from there. Bernini was contemptuous of the petit bourgeois mentality of the French and dismissed practical questions about time and cost as issues for a quartermaster, not for the world's premier artist. "Do not speak to me of anything small," he warned. Bernini was equally impertinent to the king, telling Louis, "Inasmuch as you have not seen the buildings of Italy, you have remarkably good taste."

While Louis XIV reigned, Mona Lisa was ensconced in the royal bedroom, but like all *grand' amours,* she lost her favored position when the king died. As he tired of them, Louis would retire his mistresses to a convent and move on. No green pastures for aging paramours. Mona Lisa suffered a similarly cloistered fate. After the king's death, she was moved from the royal bedroom to a darkened hideaway in Versailles. Sequestered there in the Direction des Bâtiments, she waited out the madness of the French Revolution. Neglect may have saved her from the frenzied mobs.

6

DEATH DIMINISHED LEONARDO'S LUSTER. Although it is difficult to believe today, when he enjoys the celebrity of a media star, the artist and his work were neglected for years. During his lifetime, Leonardo was recognized as a giant who "painted in such a manner as to make every valiant craftsman . . . tremble and lose heart."* But he left no da Vinci masterpiece to astound travelers on the Grand Tour of Europe. No Sistine ceiling or divine *David,* like Michelangelo. No rooms filled with frescoes, like Raphael. No magnificent basilica, like Bramante.

Leonardo's largest works were the *Last Supper* fresco, flaking from the refectory wall of Santa Maria della Grazie in Milan, and the unfinished *Battle of Anghiari,* lost when Vasari refurbished Palazzo Vecchio in Florence. The few easel paintings he completed were in private collections, and the da Vinci of the extraordinary notebooks, the empiricist, engineer, and naturalist, remained the unknown Leonardo until the nineteenth century.

Mona Lisa became little more than a footnote in art history. Locked away in the private collection of the French kings, she was never glimpsed in public. Every hundred or so years, someone took note of her. Paolo Giovio, writing about Leonardo in the sixteenth century, makes a cursory mention of the sale of the portrait to François I, but he is commenting on the extravagant price the king paid, not on the painting. A century later, on a visit to Fontainebleau in 1625, another cardinal's secretary, Cassiano dal Pozzo,† registered the first precise description of Mona Lisa. It is clear from his words that she had already received the disastrous varnishing:

> A life-size portrait on wood, half-length, of a certain Gioconda, in a carved walnut frame. This is the finest workmanship of the painter that one could see and lacks only the power of speech, for all else is there. The figure is a woman between twenty-four and twenty-six years old, looking straight ahead, not at all in the style of Greek female statues, but rather full with form and softness in the cheeks. The

---

* Vasari.
† Cassiano dal Pozzo was secretary to Francesco Cardinal Barberini, whose uncle was Pope Urban VIII. His description is in the Vatican Library.

areas around the lips and the eyes have an unattainable quality, more exquisite than anyone could hope to achieve. The hairstyle is very simple but finished. The dress is black or dark brown, but it has been treated with a varnish that has given it a dismal tone, so that one cannot make it out very well. The hands are extremely beautiful and, in short, in spite of all the misfortunes that this picture has suffered, the face and the hands are so beautiful that whoever looks at it with admiration is bewitched.

In the eighteenth century, Louis XIV's historian, André Félibien des Avaux, saw Mona Lisa at Versailles and was entranced: "Truly . . . I have never seen anything more finished or expressive. There is so much grace and so much sweetness in the eyes and the features of the face that it seems alive. . . . One has the impression that this is indeed a woman who takes pleasure in being looked at."

With these few exceptions, scant notice was taken of Mona Lisa until Napoleon arrived on the scene. By then the Louvre was in its third incarnation. The fortress turned royal palace was reconfigured as a museum during the Revolution. The idea of a public showcase to display the royal collection originated with Louis XVI. The ambitious plan seemed fitting for the birthplace of the Enlightenment, but the Revolution intervened.

The *sans culottes* seized the idea as they seized the royal family. The revolutionaries would accomplish what three hundred years of Valois and Bourbons had failed to do: complete the Louvre palace and give the king's collection to the people. The change from palace to public space was a revolutionary act and an inspired public relations coup, if somewhat late in coming. Royal collections in Austria and Germany, the Vatican, the Quirinale Palace in Rome,* the Escorial in

---

* Then the popes' summer palace, later looted and confiscated by Napoleon.

Madrid, and the Hermitage in St. Petersburg had already opened their doors to the public, although visitors to the Hermitage had to arrive in full dress because they were entering the czar's house.

To flaunt the superiority of the new order, the Louvre—renamed the Musée Français—opened on August 10, 1793, the first anniversary of the fall of the monarchy. Although only a portion of the royal collection had reached the galleries, the museum was such a popular attraction that prostitutes staked out the entrances. Though not the first national museum, the Louvre became the prototype. By the close of the nineteenth century, every major Western capital had a public art museum, and the idea was spreading to other cities in Europe and the United States. Public museums were egalitarian in name only. They were elite institutions operated by the discriminating for the discerning.

Mona Lisa was one of the last works in the royal collection to move from Versailles to the Louvre, and she did not remain there long. Shortly after she arrived in Paris, Napoleon Bonaparte became the first emperor of the French and fell captive to her smile. When he retired Josephine and married the nubile Marie-Louise of Austria in the Salon Carré to secure an heir and an alliance, his eyes may have been on Madame Lisa. He transported her to his bedroom in the Tuileries Palace along with his new bride, and he maintained her there until his defeat at Waterloo in 1815.

7

NAPOLEON BONAPARTE WAS the most notorious art thief in history. Such latter-day looters as Lord Elgin and Hermann Göring pale beside the Corsican plunderer. Napoleon charged across the Continent, conquering land and confiscating art.* When Pope Pius VI protested the wholesale looting, Napoleon took him prisoner and emptied the Vatican museums and libraries. The pillage was planned as carefully as the military campaigns. Dominique-Vivant Denon, an artist and archaeologist, accompanied Napoleon on his first Egyptian expedition and began the first serious study of Egyptology. Denon became Napoleon's museum director and assembled a squad of scholars consisting of a mathematician, a chemist, a botanist, two painters, a sculptor, and an archaeologist, who rode with the troops to choose the finest works of art and science. The soldiers called Denon *"l'oeil de l'armée"*—the eye of the army.

In the Vatican, the emperor's armies seized five hundred paintings, the Laocoön; the Apollo Belvedere; rare first editions, beautifully lettered on parchment and bound in silk with silver clasps; illuminated manuscripts of Petrarch and Ovid in Latin and Greek; Galileo's handwritten works; and exotic beasts from the papal zoo. In Venice, they commandeered the horses from the Basilica of San Marco and stole Veronese's *Wedding Feast at Cana* from the wall of San Giorgio, slicing it in half to fit it in their oxcarts. In Milan, they scooped up all the pages of the da Vinci notebooks in the Ambrosiana Library— fourteen volumes of drawings and writings, all in Leonardo's

* Napoleon stole the best art, then set up museums in many of the cities he conquered, from Madrid to Milan.

mirror script. Francesco Melzi had carefully preserved and cataloged the notebooks, but after he died in 1570, his son and heirs treated the papers cavalierly. The notebooks were divided, pages were torn out and sold, and various codices ended up in Windsor, Madrid, and Milan.

Transporting Napoleon's loot was an enormous undertaking. Canvases were rolled and secured in wax cylinders. Sculpture was packed in straw, then encased in plaster. Special cages were built for the wild animals. The Napoleonic panoply traveled by land, sea, and river barge on its triumphant journey to Paris. One hundred twenty buffalo and sixty long-horned oxen pulled the train of custom-built carts from various points in Italy to the port of Livorno on the western coast.

A letter from 1798, so laudatory that Napoleon could have dictated it, described the awe in Livorno when the cavalcade reached the port:

> The whole town came out to greet the convoy, everyone was amazed by the power of a nation which, four hundred leagues from its native soil . . . had managed to transport such a large and precious cargo across the Apennines from Rome [sic.] in order to decorate the capital of its empire. What a nation, this France, they said. So impressed were they that they called her 'THE NATION,' as if she were the only one on earth deserving the title.

Sailing from Livorno, ships loaded with the imperial plunder dodged English frigates and weathered stormy seas on the short route to Marseilles. From there, the convoy continued by barge up the Rhône, following the rivers of France north to Paris. In the capital, periodic reports on the progress of the journey heightened anticipation.

The third and grandest convoy from Napoleon's Italian Expeditions, this was the most magnificent cavalcade of art ever assembled. It reached the banks of the Seine on the morning of July 27, 1798. Its destination was the Louvre, to be renamed Musée Napoleon. The half-empty galleries soon filled with the emperor's plunder. One visitor, marveling at the quantity of masterworks, called the Louvre "this great cavern of stolen goods."

In one of history's choice ironies, Napoleon's wholesale ravishment of the art of Italy led to the rediscovery of the Renaissance wonder. Shortly after the booty reached Paris, the process of rediscovering and preserving the art and science of Leonardo began. In his villa in Lombardy, Melzi had cataloged the pages and compiled Leonardo's thoughts on painting in a book he called *Trattato della Pittura,* or *Treatise on Painting.* The book was published in Italy in 1651 and later in Germany and France, among other countries. Over the course of many years, it went into sixty-two printings in France alone, and so the da Vinci codices confiscated in Milan were of great interest to French scholars. Denon had established an excellent conservation workshop at the Louvre, and there, the enormous work of classifying, studying, copying, and publishing the notebooks began. In the mid–nineteenth century, the unknown Leonardo began to emerge from the voluminous pages. In his interesting study, *Mona Lisa: The Picture and the Myth,* Roy McMullen writes that over the next fifty years, no historical figure, with the possible exception of Jesus, received more attention than Leonardo da Vinci.

8

IN 1815, WITH NAPOLEON in exile on the Island of St. Helena, Mona Lisa returned to the Louvre. She had come through Enlightenment, Revolution, and Napoleonic heroics. Now on public view, no longer enjoyed by kings and emperors alone, she began attracting the extravagant praise of connoisseurs. Mona Lisa came to epitomize the spirit of unabashed romanticism that was spreading through Europe. She was William Wordsworth's phantom of delight, a lovely apparition—the painting that came closest to perfection.* In their Gallic effusiveness, the French Romantics made her incarnate. They took Vasari's *"più vita che la vivacità"*—more alive than life itself—to heart and added moral ambivalence. She was sweetness and perfidy and the promise of a dangerous liaison. To come under her power was to be lost in "an infinite abyss."†

The French historian Jules Michelet was the first to fall for "the gracious and smiling phantom." "Beware, *la Gioconda* is a dangerous picture," he warned. "The canvas attracts me, invades me, absorbs me; I go to it in spite of myself, like the bird to the serpent." Mona Lisa madness became a family affair. Michelet's son-in-law, Alfred Dumesnil, author of *Italian Art* (published in 1854), saw in her "brilliant beauty" a dangerous temptress. "The smile is full of attraction, but it is the treacherous attraction. . . . This so soft a look, but avid like the sea, devours."

If Michelet was smitten and Dumesnil chilled, Théophile Gautier lost his head completely. A critic, novelist, and bon vivant, Gautier became infatuated and recast the Louvre beauty as the eternal femme fatale: "If Don Juan had met Mona Lisa, he would have been saved writing on his list the names of three thousand women. He would have written but one, and the wings of his love would have refused to carry him further."

As other voices joined the impassioned chorus, Mona Lisa's reputation turned as dark as the varnish that clouds her image. Gautier's friend the author Arsène Houssaye succumbed to the

---

* Wordsworth owned a copy of Mona Lisa that was shown at the popular Manchester Exhibition of 1859. It was one of the first viewings of Mona Lisa in England. The origin and fate of the copy is something of a mystery.
† Gautier.

Gioconda enchantment—to "this divinity of the chiaroscuro whose brown gaze holds chained at her feet all the generations of men . . . so perfidiously and deliciously womanly with six thousand years of experience behind her." Assembling a team of gravediggers and clairvoyants, Houssaye went to Amboise, to the ruins of the Church of Saint Florentin where Leonardo was believed to be buried. They dug up a skull, but it was never verified as being human, let alone being Leonardo's. Although the "find" was dubious (it may well have been a cow's skull), Houssaye's words still resonate:

> [Mona Lisa] is true to life yet cannot be contemplated as if it were mere matter. As we stand before it, we feel as if alone on a mountaintop with a dizzying abyss at our feet into which we are about to fall, into which we do fall. It is the infinite abyss of a dream.

Across the Channel, the critic John Ruskin scoffed at the Gallic effusions and deplored the lady who elicited them. "Leonardo," Ruskin wrote, "depraved his inner instincts by caricature, and remained to the end of his days, a slave to an archaic smile."

To Mona Lisa's fervent lovers, Ruskin's derision dropped like a gauntlet, and a British Galahad charged into the fray. Walter Pater was a young Oxford don when he wrote the defense of Mona Lisa that made him famous. Not since Vasari had anyone written with more rapture:

> *La Gioconda* is, in the truest sense, Leonardo's masterpiece, the revealing instance of his mode of thought and work. . . . Perhaps of all ancient pictures time has chilled it least. . . . She is older than the rocks among which she sits, like the vampire, she has been dead many times and learned the secrets of the grave, and has been a diver in deep seas and keeps their fallen day about her, and trafficked for strange

webs with Eastern merchants; and as Leda was the mother of Helen of Troy, and Saint Anne the mother of Mary; and all this has been to her as the sound of lyres and flutes and lives only in the delicacy with which it has molded the changing lineaments and tinged the eyelids and the hands. The fancy of a perpetual life, sweeping together ten thousand experiences, is an old one; and modern philosophy has conceived the idea of humanity as wrought upon by, and summing up in itself, all modes of thought and life. Certainly Lady Lisa might stand as the embodiment of the old fancy, the symbol of the modern idea.

More an ardent love letter than measured art criticism, Pater's paean made Mona Lisa a love object to a generation of British public schoolboys. W. B. Yeats turned his words into a poem. Oscar Wilde said, "The picture becomes more wonderful to us than it really is and reveals to us a secret of which, in truth, it knows nothing."

While all the men around her were losing their heads, it took a woman to pierce Mona Lisa's singular attraction: "No one who has set eyes upon her for a moment can ever forget her," George Sand wrote. "What is disquieting about this image is the soul shining through, appearing to contemplate yours with lofty serenity reading into your eyes while you vainly try to read into hers."

9

HUNDREDS, IF NOT THOUSANDS, of books, articles, and academic careers were built on the twin puzzles of Mona Lisa's identity and her meaning, until a third all-consuming mystery made the old questions irrelevant: Was Mona Lisa lost forever?

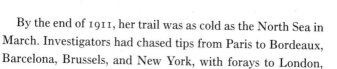
By the end of 1911, her trail was as cold as the North Sea in March. Investigators had chased tips from Paris to Bordeaux, Barcelona, Brussels, and New York, with forays to London, Madrid, Moscow, and Ghent. One lead after another evaporated. There were no new suspects, no fresh evidence.

The world intruded. Dramatic new headlines pushed the caper off the front pages:

THE UNSINKABLE *TITANIC* LOST
ON HER MAIDEN VOYAGE

SCOTT LOSES RACE TO POLE AND
DIES IN THE ATTEMPT

Without any fanfare, the blank space on the wall of the Salon Carré was filled by Raphael's portrait of Baldassare de Castiglione. It seemed a chivalrous choice. Castiglione was the author of *The Book of the Courtier,* a depiction of the ideal Renaissance prince, and in painting his portrait, Raphael was clearly influenced by the Mona Lisa he had seen on Leonardo's easel.

After so many fruitless months, public sentiment had turned from shock to sorrow, indignation to frustration, embarrassment to derision. Chorus lines made up with the face of Mona Lisa danced topless in the cabarets of Paris. Entertainers at the popular nightclub Olympia mocked the failed efforts to recover the painting. Comedians asked, "Will the Eiffel Tower be next?"

Fifteen months after her disappearance, France formally abandoned hope. In November 1912, a new deputy minister of fine arts, unscathed by the scandal,* reported to the Chamber

---

* The former minister, the beleaguered Henri-Étienne Dujardin-Beaumetz, had been forced to resign.

of Deputies: "There is no ground to hope that Mona Lisa will ever resume her place in the Louvre." The investigation officially closed.

When the new Louvre catalog was published in January 1913, *la Joconde* was no longer listed. Audaciously planned, meticulously plotted, and impeccably executed, the Mona Lisa heist seemed to be the perfect crime.

A LETTER FROM LEONARDO

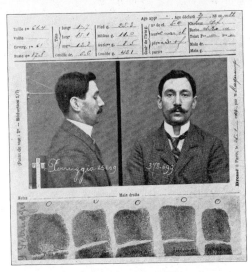

PERUGGIA MUG SHOT
The self-confessed thief, Vincenzo "Leonardo" Peruggia.
(Courtesy of Roger-Viollet/Getty Images)

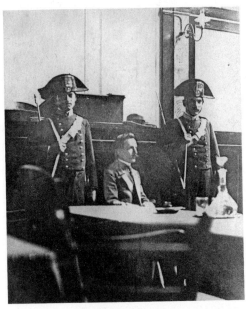

PERUGGIA IN COURT
Standing trial in Florence for the theft of Mona Lisa.
(Courtesy of Roger-Viollet/Getty Images)

I

FLORENCE IS NEVER its best in extremes. In a city that celebrates civilization as restraint, winter is rarely the finest season. It swirls down from the boney Apennines and settles in the bowl of the Arno River, creating an atmosphere as sullen and dejected as a Renaissance artist without a patron. The winter of 1913 would be the exception. Overnight, the mood of the city became euphoric, and the jubilation spread until the entire country was celebrating. No one was more surprised or delighted by the unexpected turn of events than Alfredo Geri, a dealer in art and antiques.

With his substantial presence, Geri oozed prosperity. He had a stocky build with broad shoulders, a tenor's barrel chest, and a gold watch chain looping across an ample paunch—the expansive figure of a man who spent considerable time wining and dining his clients. His elegant shop on Via Borgo Ognissanti, a short stroll from the Ponte Vecchio, had an enviable clientele. Geri furnished the villas and palazzos of Florence with choice works. Among his favored customers were Eleonora Duse, whose shadowy stagecraft made Bernhardt appear histrionic, and her *inamorato,* the mercurial novelist and showman Gabriele d'Annunzio.

Anticipating a busy Christmas season, Geri had placed an ad in a number of Italian newspapers, including *Corriere della Sera* and *La Stampa,* offering to pay generously for fine artwork.

The response was considerable, and he spent several mornings sorting through the promising and the preposterous replies. There was always a handful of letters offering to part with family "treasures"—a favorite pet stuffed and moth-eaten or a rusted nail from the True Cross. One response stood out from the rest. Dated November 29, 1913, it was postmarked Poste Restante, Place de la République, Paris, and signed "Leonardo."

At first Geri dismissed the letter as either a prank or the delusion of an unhinged person. But something about it, the terse wording, the unsophisticated sentiment, the flourish of the signature—he could not pinpoint exactly what—kept nagging. Geri reread the letter several times:

> The stolen work of Leonardo da Vinci is in my possession. It seems to belong to Italy since its painter was an Italian. My dream is to give back this masterpiece to the land from which it came and to the country that inspired it.
>
> —Leonardo.

La Gioconda had been missing from the Louvre for more than two years, and in that time, Mona Lisa look-alikes had been popping up all over Europe. The international press reported each sighting, however bogus.

Mona Lisa had been spotted crossing the border into Switzerland and slinking out of France at Le Havre and Dunkirk. She was glimpsed hopping a freight train headed for Holland by way of Namur, Liège, and Brussels, and seen boarding the steamer *Cordillera*, headed for South America. Police in Bordeaux, where the ship was docked, searched the steamer and delayed her departure but discovered no stowaway. Wrong ship, maybe. Mona Lisa was also reported boarding the S.S. *La Champagne*, bound for South America.

In August, an obviously well-to-do English gentleman had burst into the British embassy in Paris one evening with a painting that he suspected might be the missing masterpiece. The flustered ambassador immediately called in the French authorities. Mona Lisa appeared authentic down to the slight crack near the top left corner of the panel. After subjecting the painting to a minute examination, a team of experts from the Ministry of Beaux Arts and the Louvre concluded unanimously that the age was right and the quality exceptional, but the Englishman's Mona Lisa was a copy.

In September, a Russian newspaper reported that the stolen painting was hanging on the wall of a private gallery in St. Petersburg. She was sighted in New York City a few weeks later: On November 1, *The New York Times* reported that the Secret Service had staked out an apartment on the corner of Intervale Avenue in the Bronx.

It was almost inevitable that an offer for one of the false Mona Lisas would arrive in Alfredo Geri's morning mail. The dealer read the note again. When Mona Lisa disappeared, Corrado Ricci, Italy's foremost Renaissance scholar and the minister of art, had called for patience. Since the painting would be impossible to sell, Ricci had predicted, "The thief will eventually give himself away." Two years of waiting had yielded only false hope. But if the waiting were over and Geri recovered the lost da Vinci, he would be a hero and an even wealthier man. Publicity, celebrity, and many lire would be his.

Geri brought the letter to Giovanni Poggi, the director of the Uffizi Gallery. Poggi was even more skeptical. At best, the painting being offered might be a decent copy. Nevertheless, he advised Geri to write back, saying that he would have to see the painting to make an offer.

"Leonardo" answered by return mail, inviting the dealer to visit him. Geri was a prudent man, and the vision of two Italians in Paris with the kidnapped painting alarmed him. He replied with a counter-offer, asking "Leonardo" to bring Mona Lisa to Italy and suggesting Milan as an intermediate locale.

"Leonardo" was clearly impatient. He wanted to rendezvous immediately, but the dates he proposed were confusing. After a flurry of correspondence, and with a creeping sense that the affair was an elaborate prank, Geri set a firm date. They would meet in Milan in two weeks, on December 22, three days before Christmas. In the meantime, he tried to put "Leonardo" out of his mind.

On Wednesday, December 10, the shop on Via Borgo Ognissanti was unusually crowded. One customer stood out from the usual clientele. He browsed through the antiques leisurely, as if he had time to kill. After Geri had ushered out the other customers, the man introduced himself. "Leonardo" had brought Mona Lisa home to Florence.

By all accounts, the true Leonardo had been a Renaissance hunk—tall and graceful, with gracious manners. His stand-in was an entirely different type—vain, slightly unctuous, inclined to preen. Probably in his early thirties, he was a slight, edgy man, not more than five feet three inches, with a dark complexion, slick pomaded black hair, and a handlebar mustache waxed at the tips. His demeanor was ingratiating; the cut of his suit was cheap. He said that he was registered as Leonardo Vincenzo at the Albergo Tripoli-Italia on Via Panzani, a short walk away. The hotel was in the vicinity of the Borgo San Lorenzo, a few blocks from the Renaissance home where Lisa del Giocondo had sat for the true Leonardo.

Caught off guard by the unexpected turn of events, Geri asked "Leonardo" to come back the next day at three o'clock, He knew the Uffizi director was in Bologna, and he did not want to examine Mona Lisa alone. Geri immediately telegraphed Director Poggi, who rushed back to Florence. When he arrived at the shop the next afternoon at three o'clock, Geri was alone. The dealer had his gold pocket watch out and was glued to the excruciatingly slow movement of the hands. Time ticked by—five minutes, seven minutes, ten minutes.

Director Poggi had been wary from the start. Now the entire episode appeared to be one more chapter in Mona Lisa's tangled history. As he put on his coat to return to the Uffizi, "Leonardo" appeared. The director was a reserved man, not given to displays of emotion. Even with familiars, his manners were formal. "Leonardo" never hesitated. He grasped Poggi's hand in both of his and pumped it with enthusiasm, saying how glad he was to shake the hand of the man entrusted with the art treasure of Florence.

The winter light was fading when the three men began to walk together, north along Via del Moro in the general direction of Santa Maria Novella, to the Albergo Tripoli-Italia. Poggi and Geri had grown nervous waiting, and their apprehension deepened as they approached the hotel. "Leonardo" seemed oblivious. It was his first trip to Florence, and like a tourist on holiday, he sauntered along, taking in the sights around him.

At some point in the course of the afternoon, the conversation turned from art to commerce. Memories were selective and contradictory, and which man was the more honest may have been a question of degree. According to Geri, "Leonardo" raised the subject of payment before they left the shop. "'Leonardo' answered all my questions with much assurance and told me he wanted five hundred thousand lire, [equivalent to $2.14 million today] for his picture," Geri said. "I said I was prepared to pay this sum, if she was, in truth, the eternal *Gioconda*."

According to "Leonardo," Geri proposed the payment as they were walking to the hotel. While admitting that he expected the Italian government to compensate him "for the great service rendered," "Leonardo" insisted, "I did not take the picture through a desire for gain, but wished to accomplish a good and holy work by returning to my country one of the many treasures stolen from it."

Whichever account is the true one, by the time they arrived at the hotel, an agreement had been reached to ransom Mona Lisa for the sum proposed. It remained only for Director Poggi to identify her unequivocally.

The Tripoli-Italia was as shabby and shopworn as a second-hand suit, and "Leonardo's" room was on the third floor, up two steep flights. Conversation evaporated on the climb. The single room was barely large enough for a bed and an armoire, let alone three men, two of them on the portly side. As Geri and Poggi crowded in, "Leonardo" locked the door behind them and, without a word, dragged a case from under the bed. It was white wood of medium size.

In the cramped, silent room, the smallest sound seemed amplified: the bolt snapping in the door, the scrape of the case on the bare floor, the complaint of the springs as "Leonardo" heaved the box onto the bed. He opened it and began dumping out the contents, all "wretched objects," Geri would say. Woolen underwear, rumpled shirts, a pair of worn-down shoes, a squashed hat, a mandolin, and a few tools piled up on the floor. "Leonardo" had even packed some paintbrushes. When his meager possessions were strewn across the floor, he lifted a false bottom in the case. Under it was a package bundled in red silk, which he placed on the bed. Still without a word, "Leonardo" began to unwrap it.

Geri described the moment: "To our amazed eyes, the divine *Gioconda* appeared intact and marvelously preserved. We carried it to a window to compare it to a photograph we had brought with us. Poggi studied it and we had no doubt the painting was authentic. The Louvre catalogue number and brand on the back matched the photograph."

While admitting that she appeared to be the genuine article, Director Poggi expressed reservation. He would have to bring Mona Lisa back to the Uffizi and study the painting beside other works by da Vinci before he could validate its authenticity. "Leonardo" agreed without argument.

With Mona Lisa once again wrapped in her red silk mantle, Poggi and Geri carried her down the stairs. They knew they had the true Mona Lisa in their arms. Although they had contained their excitement in front of her kidnapper, they were practically running, afraid "Leonardo" would change his mind and come after them. As they fled past the front desk with their package, the concierge stopped them and insisted on seeing what they had concealed in the red silk. The thief had walked out of the Louvre carrying Mona Lisa with no questions asked, but the director of the Uffizi was stopped trying to leave the Albergo Tripoli-Italia and accused of filching a second-rate reproduction from one of the rooms. "If the guardians of the Louvre had had the same curiosity," Geri would say, "the *Gioconda* would never have come to Florence."

Once they were safely free of the hotel, Poggi called in the carabinieri. "Leonardo" was napping, his sorry belongings still in a mess on the floor, when the chief of the Florence police, Francesco Tarantelli, knocked on his hotel room door. The momentous arrest, two years in coming, was made with no fireworks. "Leonardo" submitted without a whimper. He was confident that his arrest was simply a formality. The Italian government had to put on a public show of anger, then he would be released, handsomely rewarded, and hailed as a national hero.

At the Uffizi, Director Poggi telegraphed Corrado Ricci in Rome. The Renaissance scholar and minister of art was on the next *rapida* to Florence. Together, he and Poggi examined the panel minutely. The more closely they studied it, the more excited they became. The lost Leonardo had been found. Both men would stake their reputations on it. Mona Lisa had come full circle. She was recovered in Florence, where her life began, only slightly the worse for wear. There was a bruise on one cheek and a small scratch on her left shoulder. Otherwise, she was in remarkably good shape for her four hundred years.

2

KING VICTOR EMMANUEL, Pope Pius X, and the French ambassador Camille Barrère received personal phone calls with the astounding news. In the Italian Chamber of Deputies, a fistfight was interrupted. Someone shouted: "*La Gioconda ha trovato!*"—Mona Lisa has been found!—and fisticuffs turned to *abbracci.*

Like the robbery, the recovery dominated the news:

LA GIOCONDA DI LEONARDO DA VINCI
RECUPERATA DOPO DUE ANNI
LA CONFERMA UFFICIALE

LEONARDO DA VINCI'S MONA LISA
RECOVERED AFTER TWO YEARS
CONFIRMATION IS OFFICIAL

"The lost is found!" echoed from north to south. Within twenty-four hours, *Gioconda* frenzy was electrifying Italy.

Mona Lisa's sudden reappearance was as astounding as her loss. The most famous face in the world, unseen for more than two years, had miraculously reappeared a few blocks from the house where Leonardo da Vinci had begun painting her. When the police apprehended the thief, he had a train ticket stub and a single franc in his pocket. Submitting proudly to arrest, he proclaimed himself a national savior.

"Leonardo" cooperated fully and eagerly with the police. His true identity was Vincenzo Peruggia, thirty-two years old, born on October 8, 1881, in the small town of Dumenza, near Lake Como. His Paris address was 5 Rue de l'Hôpital Saint-Louis. While the Paris police had been combing the world in search of a mastermind, a madman, or a millionaire, Mona Lisa had never strayed far from home. The divine *Gioconda,* whose address had always been one royal palace or another,* had been holed up in the heart of Paris in a cheap room, less than two miles from the Louvre and just a short distance from the Montmartre headquarters of the Picasso gang.

Peruggia was not a romantic dreamer, a young Goethe, a reincarnated Adam Lux, a rapacious American millionaire, or an avant-garde artist. Except for the fact that he had abducted Leonardo's masterpiece, Vincenzo Peruggia was a thoroughly inconsequential man, a petty crook and sometime house-painter who had worked as a glazier at the Louvre for two years, and the story he told was stranger than all the fantasies concocted to explain the heist. Peruggia portrayed himself as a patriot who had kidnapped Mona Lisa to avenge "the splendid plunder" that poured into France from the emperor Napoleon's Italian Expeditions. According to Peruggia's spurious history, Napoleon had stolen Mona Lisa from Italy, and he had stolen her back to right the wrong.

Florence was jubilant. The Albergo Tripoli-Italia changed its name to Hotel la Gioconda. Minister Ricci said, "I feel convinced that the thief did not spirit *la Gioconda* to Florence, but that it was *la Gioconda* who brought him here and has been the ravisher." An American visitor, Carolyn Apperson Leech, wrote in her diary: "The year 1913 has added another date to Florentine history. By the evening of December 12, the names of Peruggia, the thief; Signor Geri, the art dealer; Signor Poggi, Director of the Uffizi Gallery; and Commendatore Ricci, the

---

* Fontainebleau, Versailles, the Tuileries, or the Louvre.

Italian Minister of Fine Arts, were as familiar as the names of friends."

If the mood in Italy was euphoric, the mood in France was incredulous. The government, the investigators, the museum officials, the press, and the public—all were skeptical. A Louvre curator, interrupted during dinner with a phone call, responded, "Impossible!," hung up, and returned to his meal. Magistrate Drioux, for reasons sincere or self-serving, dismissed Peruggia's story out of hand. He did not accept that an Italian "macaroni" was the lone thief. "I do not believe Peruggia's story of how he stole Mona Lisa," the judge said. "It does not fit into the facts as we know them."

Of the three most involved in the investigation, Drioux was the only one still working. After twenty years, Louis Lépine had retired as prefect of the Seine the previous March, and Alphonse Bertillon was dying. The fabled criminologist had been seriously sick since October, but he was spending his final months working on a plan to end the plague of art forgery.

One of the few happy Frenchmen was the ousted Louvre director Homolle. The day after Mona Lisa's recovery, he said: "It will fill with gladness the hearts of all the true artists of the world. I believe, and I think my belief will be shared by the public, that the theft was the act of a cunning madman. His misdeed and the preposterous explanation he gives seem to prove it."

Peruggia did not appear either cunning or mad. He basked in his role as hero-thief and spoke freely and often, giving numerous interviews, detailing his motive and method:

> I was ashamed that for more than a century no Italian had thought of avenging the spoliation committed by Frenchmen under Napoleon when they carried off from Italian museums and galleries pictures, statues and treasures of all kinds by

wagonloads, ancient manuscripts by thousands, and gold by sackfulls. Many times, while working in the Louvre, I stopped before da Vinci's picture and was humiliated to see it there on foreign soil. I thought it would be a great thing for Italy were I to present the wonderful masterpiece to her, so I planned the theft.

More than one hundred years may seem a long while to hold a grudge, but history has shown again and again that collective memories are long. Italy's gripe with Napoleon was only a century old. In the context of European history, the humiliation was still fresh. If asked, "Are the French all thieves?," an Italian would invariably answer, "*Non sono tutti i francese, ma bona parte*"—not all the French are, but a Bonaparte.

Grateful Italians embraced the hero-thief as Italy's Don Quixote. Mona Lisa became his Dulcinea. An anonymous man offered to pay five thousand lire ($1,000) for Peruggia's bail, and his jail cell filled with admiring letters, gifts, cigarettes, and sweets. The poet and novelist Gabriele D'Annunzio, never one to shun the limelight, rushed into print with a tribute:

> He who dreamed of honor and grandeur; he the avenger of Napoleonic thefts; he who kept Leonardo's *la Gioconda* in Paris for two years, deceiving the French police, and then took her across the border back to Florence. Do you understand? Back to Florence where she was born, near Palazzo Vecchio, by the sounds of the bells of Giotto's campanile, able to see the cypresses of San Miniato. . . . Only a poet, a great poet, could dream such a dream.

D'Annunzio would play a bizarre and questionable role in the Mona Lisa affair. He might have been simply blowing his own horn, or he might have been a conduit in a political morality play. D'Annunzio claimed a number of roles for himself, his part changing with Mona Lisa's misadventures. In 1905 or 1906, D'Annunzio wrote a play called *La Gioconda,* in which a sculptor has an affair with his muse. In 1911, when Mona Lisa vanished, he was living in Paris at the Hôtel Meurice, and in 1913 he was living in Florence with Eleonora Duse, where they were customers of Alfredo Geri. A few days before Mona Lisa was recovered, D'Annunzio announced that *la Gioconda* would be returning to Florence. When Peruggia was arrested, D'Annunzio paid lavish tribute to the hero-thief. Later, the writer claimed that he had orchestrated both the theft and the return.

While it seems another inspired fiction, D'Annunzio evidently convinced himself that his scenario was true. In 1920 he wrote, "The sublime stealer of the Mona Lisa brought the panel, wrapped in an old horse blanket, to me in my retreat in Landes, France." The claim sounds delusional, and D'Annunzio further undermined his own strained story by claiming that Peruggia, whom the court-appointed psychiatrist would diagnose as "mentally deficient," engaged him in "metaphysical speculations" for an entire day.

3

THE FRENCH HAD DEVOURED the baron's confession implicating Apollinaire and Picasso. Now Italians were mesmerized by Peruggia's confession. They pictured the young hero-thief far from home, falling under the spell of the timeless beauty he had rescued. As Italy applauded his feat, Peruggia warmed to his story, adding romantic embellishments:

> My work as a housepainter brought me in contact with many artists. I always felt that deep in my soul I was one of them. I

spent many hours at the Louvre enjoying the masterpieces of Italy, which should never have left my country. I shall never forget the evening after I had carried the picture home. I locked myself in my room in Paris and took the picture from a drawer. I stood bewitched before *la Gioconda*. I fell victim to her smile and feasted my eyes on my treasure every evening, discovering each time new beauty and perversity in her. I fell in love with her.

Peruggia stuck to his story under intense interrogation. Insisting that the idea of avenging the Corsican bandit obsessed him, he vowed with a sense of aggrieved honor, "I would be unworthy of Italy if I did not return to her one of these masterpieces."

The Italian public was in thrall, but the Italian constabulary was not persuaded. Police chief Tarantelli was as skeptical as the French. After questioning Peruggia repeatedly, Tarantelli was convinced that the story was fictitious. Peruggia was playing a role in a script written by an anonymous playwright. It was a brilliant performance but a performance nonetheless.

The man did not match the crime, and even more curiously, his motive did not match the history. While it is true that the first emperor of France was a notorious art thief, Mona Lisa had been seducing the rulers of France long before Napoleon claimed an empire.

4

WHATEVER THE TRUTH of the tale, Mona Lisa once again became an international sensation. In Paris, extra editions of the afternoon newspapers trumpeted the find. The illustrated newspaper *Excelsior* put a photograph of the thief on its front page, encircled with sketches, like panels of a comic strip, showing each step of the theft.

In England, *The Illustrated London News* issued a special supplement with a double-page spread of the painting. For three consecutive weeks, Mona Lisa was the lead story. Even the normally circumspect London *Times* became treacly:

> *All is well that ends well, save for Vincenzo, who is still bewildered at finding his pains rewarded by prison and is convinced of an honorable release. What were really his motives, it would be hard to say. Mona Lisa, who might tell, only wears her enigmatic smile. After all, perhaps the story was one of simple enchantment and Vincenzo, who has shared a garret with Mona Lisa for two years, is not so much to be pitied.*

In the United States, the *Los Angeles Times* headlined MONA LISA IS FOUND: ITALIAN ART FANATIC CONFESSES and reported, "It is a moot question whether he is an intense patriot, a reckless thief, or insane, perhaps all three."

On the East Coast, *The New York Times* ran both a breaking-news account and an editorial on the recovery. The article began:

> *The smile of* la Gioconda, *to which the wonder and admiration of men have been directed for a dozen generations, has suffered but a momentary eclipse. The tale of her return after hope had been all but abandoned . . . will be read with a curious sense of relief, not only by those to whom art is the wellspring of life, but by countless men and women who have read in her features some faint conception of the secret of the Renaissance, some enlightenment on the meaning of good and evil in humanity. . . .*

Finding Mona Lisa was a coup for Italy, a relief for the government of France, and a stroke of luck for Alfredo Geri, who collected a reward of twenty-four thousand francs (about

$100,000 today) from *les Amis du Louvre* and received the rosette of the Légion d'Honneur from France.*

A delegation of experts, led by Paul Leprieur, curator of paintings at the Louvre, was dispatched to Florence. As luck would have it, the month before Mona Lisa was stolen, a photographic firm had taken a series of photographs of the painting, including both back and front views, for the Louvre. They were magnified and brought to Italy. Minister Ricci welcomed the second opinion, if ruefully. "I only wish that the French experts would consider it a copy," he said, "then Mona Lisa would remain in Italy."

The Louvre Mona Lisa had several identifying features. One was a vertical crack in the wood panel just to the left of the part in her hair. It probably happened soon after Leonardo finished painting, as the wood expanded and contracted. At some point, to contain the crack, strips of cloth and a pair of butterfly wedges were glued to the back of the panel. When Mona Lisa was recovered in Florence, only one butterfly was in place, but the position of the wedges was clear.

Another defining feature was the *craquelure*. Skeptics might argue that the Louvre labels could be faked, but Leonardo himself could not reproduce with absolute accuracy each minute fissure. Various causes—old age, the effect of varnishes, and the way the original layers of paint were applied—can result in a distinct network of fine cracks on the surface of a painting. After comparing photographs of the Louvre Mona Lisa and the recovered work inch by inch, Curator Leprieur validated the find.

As soon as Mona Lisa's authenticity was verified, the government of Italy issued an official statement:

---

* Geri was not happy with his reward. He sued for 10 percent of the value of the painting. His claim was rejected.

The Mona Lisa will be delivered to the French ambassador with a solemnity worthy of Leonardo da Vinci and a spirit of happiness worthy of Mona Lisa's smile. Although the masterpiece is dear to all Italians as one of the best productions of the genius of their race, we will willingly return it to its foster country, which has regretted its loss so bitterly, as a pledge of friendship and brotherhood between the two great Latin nations.

With France a member of the Triple Entente and Italy of the Triple Alliance, relations had been antagonistic. Italy's gracious response to Mona Lisa's recovery warmed the atmosphere between the nations, but it angered many ordinary Italians. There was a general feeling throughout Italy that if Mona Lisa were returning to the Louvre, France should reciprocate by sending back some of the art that Napoleon really had stolen.

5

THE RECOVERY OF Mona Lisa by the Italians was a public mortification for the French investigators. Vincenzo Peruggia should have been a prime suspect. He had been living in Paris since 1908, and for several of those years, up until January 1911, he had been employed at the Louvre. He was one of the glaziers who had constructed Mona Lisa's controversial glass-enclosed frame. Since he had put her in the frame, he knew better than anyone how to remove her.

Peruggia was on the list of present and past museum employees that Louvre officials provided to the police. He had been summoned for questioning in the case, and when he failed to appear, a detective went to his apartment, searched it, and interrogated him. Peruggia said that he was at work on the morning of August 21. If the police had checked his alibi, they would have found that he arrived at his job several hours late and told his boss that he had overslept, but his alibi was never corroborated, and he was never fingerprinted. Everyone from the Louvre director to the lowliest workman, it seems, had been fingerprinted—except the thief.

Even those glaring oversights should not have mattered, because Peruggia had a rap sheet. He had been arrested twice in France, which meant that the French police had his criminal profile in their system. On June 23, 1908, Peruggia had been charged with attempted robbery and spent the night in jail in Mâcon, near Lyons. In Paris a few months later, he was involved in a fight over a prostitute. Because he was carrying a knife, he was arrested for weapons possession, sentenced to eight days, and fined sixteen francs.

Alphonse Bertillon had a full criminal profile of Vincenzo Peruggia in his files, two sets of mug shots, two sets of fingerprints, and the thumbprint lifted from Mona Lisa's frame, yet Peruggia's profile never turned up. Although Bertillon had reputedly the most sophisticated organization in Europe, with seven hundred fifty thousand criminal records cataloged and cross-referenced, they were classified only by right prints. The impression on Mona Lisa's frame was a left thumbprint and could not be matched.

The French police had Mona Lisa in their sights from the beginning, but no one realized it. Their fixation on a ring of art thieves had narrowed their perspective. After Peruggia's arrest, a new team of investigators scrambled to gather the evidence that Lépine and Bertillon had missed. The renewed hunt started with Peruggia's apartment.

Photographs show a dingy room with an unmade brass bed and an old gas stove. Soiled floral wallpaper covers the walls of the closet where Mona Lisa was stashed. The closet is empty except for a pile of trash and an old umbrella. The police came away with a sheaf of ninety-three love letters and a daybook suggesting the thief's motives might not have been as pure as he pretended. Currency, not Napoleon, had been on Peruggia's mind from the outset. A journal entry dated December 10, 1910, eight months before the heist, listed the names of art collectors and dealers in the United States, Italy, and Germany, including John D. Rockefeller, J. P. Morgan, Andrew Carnegie, and Alfredo Geri.

The love letters Peruggia had saved were written in fractured French, probably by a foreigner, the police thought, and signed Mathilde. Immediately, word of a mythic romance spread. As the story was recounted, Peruggia had fallen desperately in love with the beautiful Mathilde, who bore an uncanny resemblance to Mona Lisa. Mathilde was killed, and unable to have the flesh-and-blood woman, the heartbroken young lover took her image instead.

In a somewhat more circumspect account, *The New York Times* reported that Peruggia had met Mathilde in a Paris dance hall. She had come with another Italian and was injured in a fight. Rushing to her rescue, Peruggia carried her to a cab and brought her to the home of an old Italian woman who nursed her back to health. During her convalescence, friendship turned to ardent love.

While continuing to hunt for the mysterious Mathilde, police also searched the apartments of Peruggia's neighbors and friends. Although initially he insisted that he had acted alone, under questioning, Peruggia implicated two brothers, Vincente and Michele Lancelotti. It was one of the few inconsistencies in his account. The Lancelottis were "macaroni," too, and according to Peruggia, they hid the picture and helped him construct the false-bottomed box.

Within the week, the brothers and a certain Mathilde Clamagirand were under arrest. All three denied any knowledge of Mona Lisa or her kidnapping. Mathilde did not recall ever seeing Mona Lisa or even hearing Peruggia murmur her name, although she did remember the white case in his room.

In Florence, Peruggia continued to glory in his fame. He scoffed at the Paris investigators and mocked their scenario of the theft. Instead of slinking out the side entrance at the Porte Visconti, as the French investigators surmised, Peruggia boasted that he had carried Mona Lisa in his arms down the front stairs of the Louvre. With a salute to the *Winged Victory,* he marched out the front gate. No one questioned him or tried to impede him in any way. On that bright August morning, the thief and his captive strolled home, where he deposited her in his apartment, then went to work.

Peruggia's boast conflicted with the testimony of the Louvre plumber Sauve and with the evidence. The brass doorknob, missing from a side entry, had been recovered in the museum garden near the Porte Visconti. But after so many slights and resentments, belittled as a "macaroni," he was evening the score. "The abstraction of the picture was a very simple matter. I had only to choose an opportune moment and a mere twist would put the picture in my hands. The idea took possession of me, and I decided to take the step." Peruggia expressed great happiness that he had finally restored da Vinci's masterpiece to Florence, where it belonged. "I am an Italian and I do not want the picture given back to the Louvre," he said. "It must hang in the Uffizi Gallery." Peruggia's wish was answered, if only briefly.

6

ONCE THE LOUVRE TEAM confirmed that the recovered art was the real da Vinci, a grateful France, at the request of

Minister Ricci, allowed Mona Lisa to stay in her homeland for two weeks. Protected by an international honor guard of gendarmes and carabinieri in full dress uniform, she made her debut in the Uffizi Gallery on December 14. Mona Lisa was decked out in a carved and gilded sixteenth-century walnut frame and carried through the corridors with the solemnity of a canonization. Government officials, artists, journalists, and dignitaries gathered for the triumphant procession. It was an emotional moment. Soldiers saluted, men doffed their hats, and women made the sign of the cross as she passed.

Mona Lisa was brought into the portrait gallery, where Florentines who had known Leonardo and Lisa del Giocondo looked down from their frames. There, on a stage draped in velvet and protected by a railing, she was placed on an easel between Leonardo's *Annunciation* and the *Adoration of the Magi*.

Carolyn Leech described the scene in her diary:

> The picture in profound silence moved down the long corridor. The silence was reverent as if the audience were in veneration. . . . High officials of the army there were, and men of lowest rank, artists of all degrees and artisans, the titled world and scholars, the working world and peasants. . . . Not even the hanging of the Baptistery's first bronze door could have stirred the emotions much more deeply than did this procession, at once so medieval and so modern. . . .
>
> Suddenly, as in a flash, one understood that the lovely Tuscan scene, the background for the mysterious lady, was a prophecy fulfilled—had she not traveled the distance across the mountains and followed the road by the river until she reached home? Much is written of "the darkened condition" of the canvas. . . . Perhaps the dimness of the two-year hiding place had rested the centuries-old colors, young when America was young. If there remains not the first glory, in its place shines a transfiguring new light.

The Italians were crazed with joy. An ecstatic throng estimated at more than thirty thousand had gathered outside the
Uffizi. Groups of one hundred, women first, were allowed to
enter. Director Poggi manned the door of the gallery, urging
calm, but the crowd swept past the guards and mobbed the
museum to glimpse their *Gioconda*. The stampede threatened
to topple busts and statues. Police were knocked aside and
windows broken in the wild rush to reach her.

After five days at the Uffizi, with the fifth and final day
reserved for schoolchildren and their teachers, Mona Lisa
went on the road. She became history's first traveling mega art
show. Minister Ricci, who had remained in Florence with her,
organized the trip and personally supervised her packing in a
custom-fitted padded rosewood box with a lock and key.

On the morning of December 20, protected by a police
guard, Ricci, Director Poggi, and several parlor cars of officials
escorted Mona Lisa by train to Rome. Carabinieri were on
alert at every station along the route, just as they were when
the royal family traveled. In Rome, King Victor Emmanuel
enjoyed a private viewing. On December 21, 1913, at another
solemn ceremony befitting a coronation or an abdication,
Mona Lisa was officially returned to France. She was placed in
the hands of the French ambassador Camille Barrère, who
brought her to Palazzo Farnese, which had become the French
embassy. While she was in residence there, the queen of Italy,
the queen mother, and the entire diplomatic corps came to call.

Mona Lisa spent Christmas in Rome. For five days, from
Tuesday through Saturday, she was on exhibit at the Borghese
Gallery. Security was stringent. There was fear that Peruggia
had not been a lone thief and that his accomplices would stop
at nothing to get Mona Lisa back. A police phalange surrounded her at all times, and Minister Ricci was at her side
during museum hours. Plainclothes detectives mingled with

the crowds. On the final day, the throng was so large that women fainted and extra police were called out. Even after the gallery closed for the night, Romans kept a vigil at the gate.

From Rome, Mona Lisa traveled to Milan. Again, the crowds were enormous and enormously enthusiastic. For two days, she held court at the Brera Gallery, and no one remembered, or cared to remember, that the Brera had been founded by Napoleon. A commemorative medal struck to mark the occasion bore the head of Leonardo da Vinci and the inscription "May her divine smile ever shine." On her final night in Italy, the gallery stayed open until midnight to accommodate a crowd of sixty thousand.

There were no *arrivedercis*—see you again—only *addio*. This was *la Gioconda*'s last goodbye to her homeland. She had traveled in state from Florence to Rome, and from Rome to Milan, and wherever she went, adoring throngs greeted her. After her triumphant two-week tour, she was carefully packed for her return to France. Again escorted by a delegation of politicians, museum officials, and police guards, she was given a private train car on the Milan-Paris express. Mona Lisa, who had spent two ignominious years closeted in a grungy Paris apartment and then had traveled in third class across Europe, was going home in grand style. The masterpiece that Napoleon did *not* steal was on its way back to rejoin the imperial booty.

7

AT THREE O'CLOCK on New Year's Eve morning, the Milan-Paris express crossed the border and entered France. It reached the Gare de Lyon at two-thirty that afternoon.

Paris was dressed for the holidays. The mood was festive,

and there was frost in the air. Mona Lisa was everywhere, smiling from cards and posters. In Paris that Christmas, there were more pictures of Mona Lisa than the Holy Family. The Louvre issued a formal card, announcing that she would be receiving visitors again every day except Monday. Another popular, if ruder, postcard pictured her with a baby in her arms and Peruggia's face in the upper-left corner. The caption read *Son Retour*—Her Return.

The lakes and ponds in the Bois de Boulogne and the lagoon at Versailles were frozen solid. So, too, were the expressions of the chic Parisians. In Paris society, the "Mona Lisa look" was all the fad. There was a run on yellow powder, which, dusted generously on the face, neck, and bust, suggested her golden complexion. Society ladies practiced her smile, which immobilized their facial muscles and consequently minimized conversation.

Although anticipation was keen, Mona Lisa did not go directly to the Louvre. Like a prisoner of war who has been repatriated or rescued, she was "debriefed." At the École des Beaux-Arts, she was examined, X-rayed, photographed, and subjected to a minute analysis of her *craquelure*. In her column for *Le Matin,* Colette deplored the experience: "They pick at her, uncover her, discover her."

Finally, on January 4, 1914, Paris officially welcomed Mona Lisa home. A gala procession transported her through the streets. Refitted in her old carved frame, she returned to the Louvre at last, but not to her familiar spot in the Salon Carré. In her first two days back, one hundred thousand visitors streamed in to see her, twenty times the usual number. Because the crowds were so huge, she was temporarily given a gallery of her own.

Mona Lisa left the Louvre a work of art. She returned an icon. The private seduction of Walter Pater had become the public seduction of the masses.

8

IN AUGUST 1911, when Mona Lisa vanished, *The New York Times* predicted:

Whoever it was who stole Leonardo da Vinci's la Gioconda or Mona Lisa from the Louvre is sure of a place in history when his name comes out. He is sure of an extraordinary place, too. It is not possible to locate the general who fought the greatest battle since the world was made, or the statesman who framed the greatest law, or the author who wrote the greatest book; but it will always be possible henceforth to locate the thief who committed the greatest theft.

The opposite proved true. Vincenzo Peruggia was not brought to trial until June 4, 1914, and by then the drama had played out. *La Gioconda* had moved on, and Florentines had moved on, too. After the first euphoric flush, spontaneous outpourings of awe and affection waned. No more gifts of cigarettes and *dolci* for Peruggia. Mona Lisa was back in Paris and hanging safely in her old spot, surrounded on all sides by Napoleon's plunder. Without her luminous glow, Vincenzo Peruggia was on his own, parading before the world in the emperor's new clothes. It was not a prepossessing sight.

Whether he was Mona Lisa's abductor or her savior, Peruggia was a disappointment. In the pantheon of great criminals real or imaginary, he was an embarrassment. Peruggia was not a suave escape artist in white tie and tails, like Adam Worth, who spirited away Gainsborough's *Duchess of Devonshire* under the nose of Scotland Yard. He was not a cerebral nemesis like Professor James Moriarty, "the Napoleon of crime," who matched wits with Sherlock Holmes. He was not even the shrewdly elusive Flambeau, "the colossus of crime who ran down the Rue de Rivoli with a policeman under each arm," whom Father Brown was forever tailing. If Peruggia had arrived twenty years later, he could have played the comic foil in the frothy musicals of Fred Astaire and Ginger Rogers ("Sono Tonetti. It rhymes with spaghetti").

The stunning denouement had dwindled into tawdry melodrama, and the final act was an anticlimax. By the time Peruggia came to trial, Prefect Lépine had been retired for more than a year, and Alphonse Bertillon was dead. France did not press for harsh treatment. The government did not want to resurrect memories of the botched investigation or make the thief a martyr in Italy. France had not even prosecuted Peruggia's accomplices, citing a lack of evidence. Without French pressure, Italy was loath to be too severe with the man who had brought Mona Lisa home, at least for a surprise visit. Relations between the two countries were more cordial than they had been in some time, although the warm feelings would be short-lived.

A psychiatrist appointed by the court to determine Peruggia's mental state testified that he was exceedingly dumb. "Dumb like a fox" would have been more apt. The Italian investigators had amassed convincing evidence against him. They had gone to his hometown near Como, questioned his father and brothers, and discovered that his motive was less than pure. Before the theft, he had boasted to his family that he would soon be a rich man. The prosecution also uncovered evidence that Peruggia had tried to sell the portrait several times. Before contacting Geri, he had approached the London dealer Joseph Duveen, the American millionaire-collector J. P. Morgan, and art brokers in Paris and Naples. Not one of them had alerted the police. Later, Duveen admitted, "I would sooner have gone around with a stick of dynamite in my pocket for the rest of my life than have had any knowledge of that affair." Morgan, who protested so vociferously that he had never been offered Mona Lisa, had died the previous year.

In spite of the evidence against him, Peruggia kept to his part, never deviating from the script, if script there was. He put on another flawless performance as "the avenger of Italy's wrongs." Looking confident but modest in a gray suit, winged collar, and black tie, he took the witness stand and, with an attitude of aggrieved innocence, told his story to the judge.

The misadventure began at about seven o'clock on the morning of August 21, 1911, when Peruggia presented himself at the door of the Louvre with the other workmen, wearing his white smock:

> One morning I joined my fellow decorators at the Louvre, exchanged a few words with them, and quietly stole away. I was wearing the same long white workman's blouse as they did and attracted no attention and was asked no questions. I managed to get to the Salon Carré without being seen. The room was deserted. There hung the painting that is one of our great works. Mona Lisa smiled down on me. In a moment, I had snatched her from the wall. I carried her to the staircase, took off the frame, slipped the painting under my blouse, and left *con la più grande disinvoltura*—with the greatest nonchalance. It was all done in a few seconds.

Peruggia never budged from his story line when the judge cross-examined him.

"Why did you commit the theft?"

"All the Italian paintings which are in the Louvre have been stolen."

"Where did you find this out?"

"From books and photographs."

Peruggia's answer seemed canny. The idea that he had spent his free time poring over art-history books in the Bibliothèque Nationale required a willed suspension of disbelief. The judge questioned him on his alleged motive:

"Why did you write to tell your family you had finally made your fortune?"

"Romantic words, Your Honor" was his cool reply.

"Why sell her if your motive was altruistic?"

"I was anxious to ensure a comfortable old age for my parents. Besides that, I felt I must take myself away from the influence of that haunting smile. I sometimes wondered in those two and a half years whether or not I should burn the picture, fearing I should go mad."

"But you tried to sell the painting in London," the judge countered.

"This is a misunderstanding." Peruggia made the correction firmly, without betraying any hint of rancor. "In London, I went to the shop of an antiques dealer for advice on how to return Mona Lisa to Italy. The dealer did not take me seriously. He said I surely must be speaking of a copy, and I left. Had I wished to sell the painting, I would not have gone to the trouble that I did. I took the painting for Italy, and I wanted it returned to Italy. I waited until the tumult from the newspapers had quieted down before coming to Italy."

Henry Duveen had told a very different story, and the judge continued to question Peruggia's motive.

"How did you get the idea to propose the sale to the art dealer Geri?"

"While reading a newspaper, my eye caught his name, and so I thought of turning to him to make a gift of *la Gioconda* to Italy."

"Gift? But when you first met him, you proposed getting a payment of five hundred thousand lire from the Italian government."

"Who says this? Geri?" Peruggia snapped back. "It was he who suggested getting five hundred thousand, and we would share the money. He told me to ask Poggi for the money and to stick to this amount."

Peruggia's outburst seemed the most genuine moment in his testimony. The judge pressed further.

"Why did you offer the painting to a dealer rather than to the director of the Uffizi Gallery?"

"I didn't think."

"Did you expect a reward from the Italian government?"

"Certainly. I heard talk of millions, and I expected that Italy would present me with something which, for a modest family such as mine, would have been a fortune."

Peruggia, only momentarily off-script, returned to his by now familiar role as an aggrieved man, misunderstood and maligned, but neither bitter nor bowed. Either he had come to believe his own fiction or a fiction that had been fed to him, or he was a consummate actor. A series of witnesses followed.

The psychiatrist testified that he had examined Peruggia intensely over several months to determine his degree of culpability. Because the accused was "intellectually deficient," he was only partly responsible for his actions, the psychiatrist said. Police chief Tarantelli described Peruggia's previous efforts to sell the painting and repeated the boasts he had made to his family. Uffizi director Poggi described Peruggia's "quiet and calm" demeanor when he turned over the painting. Geri, the last to take the stand, recounted their negotiations.

As each witness testified, Peruggia listened with the same apparent lack of concern that he had displayed when he surrendered the painting. The *Rome Tribune* reported:

> *To observe him, one would think he had nothing to do with the trial. He displayed temper when he felt the witnesses were not testifying accurately. But it was a superficial display. Not for one moment was he disturbed. He has taken part in the debate, speaking at some length and speaking*

frankly, expressing himself in well-chosen phrases, punctuating his words with moderate and gentlemanly gestures. His words always give the impression of sincerity. Either he has never believed that he committed a crime, or he has indulged so much in autosuggestion that he has lost all sense of the importance of it.

In his closing argument, the prosecutor described a clever crime committed by a convicted felon for personal gain, not for the glory of Italy. Citing Peruggia's two convictions in France, he asked for a minimum three-year sentence.

Peruggia's lawyers, Renzo Carena and Ferdinando Targetti, each gave a summation. One argued that the trial was illegal. Italy had no jurisdiction because the crime had been committed in a foreign country, and since France never asked for his extradition, Peruggia should be a free man.

The other made an emotional appeal to all Italians. Peruggia was a loving son who had been forced to seek work in a hostile country to help his family. In France, he had been ridiculed as a "macaroni," his tools were stolen, and his wine was salted—all because he was Italian. His history might be flawed, but his heart was true. He believed Napoleon had stolen Mona Lisa, and he was avenging the dishonor. Peruggia should be returned to his family, just as he had returned *la Gioconda* to her homeland. He was not a professional thief. In fact, his actions after the theft were so stupid, they proved the psychiatrist's diagnosis that he was intellectually deficient.

The defense concluded with a stirring plea: "By accepting our conclusions, you will have listened to the voices that are coming from every part of Italy, where there is nobody who desires the condemnation of the accused." As the defense rested, the spectators exploded in wild applause, and Peruggia wept. The court adjourned until the following day.

When the trial resumed in the morning, the courtroom was

overflowing. The sympathy of the Italian public was aroused once more, but the jurors were unmoved. After deliberating for just two hours, they found Vincenzo Peruggia guilty as charged. He was sentenced to one year and fifteen days.

According to one newspaper report, the thief listened to his sentence with a smile as enigmatic as Mona Lisa's. As he was led out of the courtroom in handcuffs, he was overheard saying, "It could have been worse."

Six weeks later, the defense attorneys appealed his sentence. During those few weeks, the political climate in Europe had changed dramatically. Archduke Franz Ferdinand, heir presumptive to the Austro-Hungarian throne, was assassinated in Sarajevo. France sympathized with the Serbs, Italy with the Austrians, and the warm feelings between the countries evaporated.

Peruggia's attorneys argued that no one had been hurt by the Mona Lisa affair, and many had been helped. The painting had been returned safely and in excellent condition, the Italians had enjoyed a brief encounter with *la Gioconda,* and the French had been shown how poorly their art was protected.

On July 28, Austro-Hungary declared war on Serbia. It was the first salvo of World War I. The next day, Vincenzo Peruggia's case was closed. His sentence was reduced to seven months and nine days. Because of time served, he was released immediately, and in some confusion. The Mona Lisa thief was in an unfamiliar city and penniless once more—he turned out the pockets of his trousers to prove it as he left the courtroom. With no idea what to do or where to go, Peruggia returned to the scene of his arrest. At the front door of the Albergo Tripoli-Italia, now the Hotel la Gioconda, Mona Lisa smiled at "Leonardo" again. Her likeness was painted on the wall at the entrance with a sign: HERE *LA GIOCONDA* WAS RECOVERED.

Peruggia eventually returned home to Dumenza, where he

was welcomed as a hero. He joined the Italian army, serving honorably through the war. In 1921 Peruggia married, moved back to France, and opened a paint store in Haute-Savoie. He died on October 8, 1925, his forty-fourth birthday, leaving a wife and baby daughter.

Today, a soaring art market and the continuing problem of museum security have made art theft the third most prevalent crime in the world, surpassed only by international smuggling and drug trafficking. The risk is small, the potential gain is tremendous, and if the thief is caught, the punishment is still minimal.

Vincenzo Peruggia, aka Leonardo, served less than a year for pulling off the most audacious art heist in history. He never committed another crime, and he never confessed who was behind the pinch felt round the world. But the idea that he was the lone thief seems implausible.

A guest worker in France, unsophisticated and not very bright, with a couple of minor scrapes on his police blotter, masterminds the art theft of the ages. For more than two years, he makes only desultory efforts to capitalize on his crime. At first the thief says he acted alone, and then he implicates two accomplices, simple men much like himself. Although he is briefly lionized, he leaves jail without enough lire to buy a cappuccino and never attempts another theft. Is this the modus operandi of a master criminal?

Peruggia was a good housepainter, but he had no education and no knowledge of art. Where were the books about Napoleon and his plundering? None were found in Peruggia's apartment or in his travel case, and it is absurd to imagine the semiliterate Italian in the Bibliothèque Nationale, poring over history tomes written in French. Peruggia's own family never believed he stole Mona Lisa alone. Someone had incited him to commit the crime with the promise of wealth or the lure of patriotism.

World War I swept the Mona Lisa caper off the front pages, still the story begged for more. Years later, a journalist for the Hearst flagship paper, the *New York Journal,* provided it.

THE STING

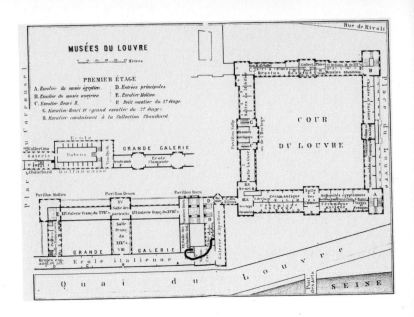

FLOOR PLANS OF THE LOUVRE

These plans of the second (premier étage) and ground (rez-de-chaussée)
floors of the Louvre show the probable route of the thieves.
X marks the spot where the missing doorknob was recovered.
Just beyond to the left and across the river is Gare d'Orsay.

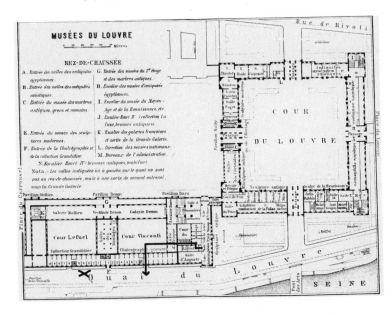

I

NEW YEAR'S 1914. Snow blanketed southern Europe, and icy blasts swept over the Mediterranean, sending a chill across the top of Africa. In the unseasonably bitter January, in a café in Casablanca, an elegant adventurer and a buccaneer journalist renewed their acquaintance. The chance of turning a dishonest penny had brought the Marqués Eduardo de Valfierno to Casablanca. A rumor of war had brought Karl Decker.

Because of its strategic location at the entrance to the Mediterranean, Morocco had become a playing field where the major powers of Europe contended for influence and advantage. German gunboats were threatening French dominance, and Decker, a star reporter for William Randolph Hearst's *New York Journal,* had come itching for a new war to cover.

Decades before Rick's Place, Casablanca was an anything-goes town where the odds of a knife at the throat or a kiss on each cheek were fifty-fifty. A chance encounter with an old acquaintance, even one whom you might otherwise hold at arm's length, seemed a stroke of good fortune. Since one or both would be gone in a day or so and never be seen again, truth could be revealed without consequence.

The two men took a table on the cobblestone terrace of a pocket-size restaurant midway between the seaside and the city hall, the Arab quarter just behind them. They angled themselves with considerable care to catch the direct sun. For added warmth, each cradled a snifter of Napoleon brandy. A French newspaper lay open on the table between them—*Le Matin* of January 4, 1914.

Through the years, their paths had crossed in other unruly, no-questions-asked places where opportunism flourished, danger was a constant, and crime paid handsomely. Decker knew the self-anointed marqués as a confidence man with a taste for high life and fine art, and after the usual exchange of pleasantries, their conversation turned to the headlined story: MONA LISA RETURNS TO THE LOUVRE.

"You know I have always been deeply interested in art," Eduardo de Valfierno began, speaking with the elegance and insouciance that was his trademark. "I have always felt that the man who made two great pictures bloom where there had been only one before was a benefactor of mankind." He paused, allowing Decker time to appreciate the irony. "You understand, of course, Mona Lisa was not stolen to be sold. The painting only appeared to be the prize to Vincenzo Peruggia's elementary mind."

At thirty-eight, Decker was a veteran of the rough-and-tumble newspaper wars of New York, and he considered his companion curiously. The Mona Lisa thief was in jail and the lost Leonardo was back in the Louvre, yet the marqués seemed to be suggesting that the case was still not closed. With his leonine head raised to the sun, Valfierno exuded the well-being of a man who was immensely pleased with himself. They made a roguish pair—the journalist-adventurer on the beat of a front-page story and the seasoned scam artist. Both were inveterate opportunists and exemplars of their professions.

Built like a battleship and sporting an extravagant mustache and a trademark fedora with a brim the width of Texas, Decker personified the swashbuckling correspondent who never allowed the facts to stand in the way of a good story.

Dubbed "a modern D'Artagnan" for his daring exploits in pursuit of front-page stories, he was as subtle as a banner headline and as inventive as his country. Decker's name made headlines almost as often as bylines. Like the Dumas musketeer, he dashed from escapade to exploit, breathlessly pursuing Hearst's "journalism of action"—rescuing a beautiful Cuban revolutionary from prison, embedding with the first landing force in the Spanish-American War, mapping an expedition to free the wrongfully accused Captain Alfred Dreyfus from Devil's Island.

The debonair marqués, every inch the gentleman thief, had patrician manners and no morals. A born aristocrat, he was the scion of a prominent family in Latin America, but if presented with a choice between an honest occupation and a clever scam, he would not suffer a moment of indecision. He was courtly, charming, and compulsively crooked.

Valfierno had been operating beyond the law without interference on three continents for years. Occasionally, he was forced to leave a country sooner than planned, but there wasn't so much as a smudge on his record. His dossier was the only immaculate thing about him. The marqués performed with blithe unscrupulousness. An amused contempt for what he called "the squirming hordes of saps in the world" and impeccable breeding gave him an aura of invincible superiority. Although he had worked many cons in his time, in these later years, he would not entertain any operation that promised less than a $50,000 profit, roughly $750,000 today.

If you believe there is honor among thieves, then you can believe that a bargain was struck on that wintry day in Casablanca. Assured that his part would not be made public in his lifetime, and safely beyond the law, the Marqués Eduardo de Valfierno confessed to a deception that he boasted was unparalleled "in insolence and ingenuity."

Perhaps like every artist, he wanted his work to be appreciated. Maybe he was in a reflective mood, or maybe with so many frauds on his conscience, he was moved to come clean—if not to purge his soul, then to satisfy his ego. Valfierno was old for the game, although he showed no inclination to retire. Whatever his motive, the marqués knew that Karl Decker would appreciate the beauty of an artful swindle. Defenses lowered and tongues loosened, conversation flowed freely. With the pride of an artist admiring his masterwork, Valfierno revealed how and why Mona Lisa had vanished.

2

THE MARQUÉS HAD a receptive audience in Karl Decker. A dozen years before, they had met in Buenos Aires, where Eduardo de Valfierno's legitimate name was so respected that it would open every door. Even though he was the youngest son in a society where the bulk of the inheritance went to the eldest, his patrimony offered unlimited opportunity. But he never used his true name, and he never revealed it in his various business ventures. Among his less nefarious interests, the marqués was something of a connoisseur, and an opportune meeting with a French art restorer had led him into the highly fluid, often questionable fine-arts market.

Yves Chaudron was described as a pale wisp of a Frenchman, almost a skeleton in his skinniness. He had begun his professional life as a painter, but lacking any creative instinct, he had drifted into art restoration, then into the considerably more profitable field of art falsification. It was a natural progression and his true calling. Few, if any, forgers could imitate art with greater mastery. Given a painting to be copied, Chaudron could capture the slightest quirks of the artist, duplicate the finest brushstrokes, and match even damaged colors. His skill was described as "the uncanny sort that breaks the heart of the collector."

Chaudron became the marqués's partner in crime and his alter ego. Valfierno was the front, Chaudron the talent. Together, they "enriched the Argentine" with the works of the popular nineteenth-century painter Bartolomé Murillo. Like Picasso, Murillo was Andalusian, but beyond a shared nationality, the two were antithetical. Murillo painted sweet Madonnas, hated by Picasso, loved by Latin widows.

In those early days, the marqués would start every morning with a stack of newspapers, circling each black cross that announced the death of a prosperous Argentinean. As a rule of thumb, the longer the obituary, the richer the deceased. Valfierno was, of course, the soul of tact when he approached a grieving widow. He would suggest that she buy a Murillo and donate it to the Church as a memorial to her dearly departed. It would be a rare and beautiful tribute. As fast as Chaudron could paint the fakes, Valfierno palmed them off. Soon they were turning out so many "genuine" Murillos that their operation became a factory.

Chaudron had learned a number of tricks from his restoration work, and in their Buenos Aires plant, electric fans whirled on the freshly varnished canvases, breaking the surfaces into thousands of tiny cracks. Vacuum cleaners operated in reverse, blowing clouds of dust on the varnish. Chaudron and his assistants added finely ground coffee to the dust, sprinkling the grains over the canvases to reproduce the flyspecks that often deface old works.

Although business was booming, the marqués was always prowling for bigger game, and he began dabbling in finance. When a syndicate that he organized began to collapse, he left

Buenos Aires expeditiously, taking an estimated quarter million dollars in gold bullion with him. Chaudron followed soon after, leaving the Argentine with more Murillos than cattle.

Sometime later, Decker bumped into the pair again in Mexico. Although they were still working the Murillo market, they had a new and riskier operation. Instead of returning to the manufacture of paintings, they were selling the same celebrated work over and over to well-heeled tourists. The scam was transparent and successful. Buyers would be offered a famous Murillo that hung in a museum in Mexico City. Seeing it on the museum wall validated its authenticity. Buyers asked few questions, hoping ignorance would insulate them from whatever unsavory activity was involved, and they would return home to await delivery. In due course, the Murillo would arrive, along with a batch of newspaper clippings, all undated. A typical lead read: "Yesterday, an outrage occurred and a priceless Murillo was ripped from its frame. . . ." If a buyer returned to Mexico City and saw the original still in the museum, the marqués would say that to avoid embarrassment, the museum was passing off a copy as the true work.

While the money was easy, painting and peddling the same canvas grew boring. Valfierno was soon looking for a new source of income to finance his indulgent lifestyle, and Chaudron had grown nostalgic for his native France. Filthy with money, the partners sailed for Paris, where they insinuated themselves easily into the carnival that was the Parisian art world. For a few unrestrained years in the afterglow of the Belle Époque, the passion for collecting rivaled the Renaissance. Corots, Millets, and even Titians were being sold in Paris every year, many of them fakes.

By 1911 the fleecing of American millionaires was a cottage industry in Europe. "All the great European fakers worked with an eye on the rich Americans. . . . The more fantastically untrue a story connected with a picture or work of art, the more likely it was to find an eager buyer among the flocks of rich Americans who vied with each other in buying the bed Queen Elizabeth (or Empress Josephine, or Cleopatra—or all three) had slept in."*

Many towns boasted their own forger. In Siena, an art restorer named Icilio Federico Ioni manufactured original paintings from the Quattrocento. In Modena, a painter aptly named Malatesta produced Titians on demand. And in Paris, after years spent cranking out perfect Murillos, the adroit Yves Chaudron turned to a more lucrative Renaissance master.

The marqués and his master forger were at the right place at the right time with the right experience to hatch the most brazen art swindle ever attempted. They would sell Mona Lisa not once but six times. It was a classic sting, elegant in its simplicity. Chaudron would paint six Mona Lisas. Valfierno would steal the original and sell each forgery to a millionaire collector as the authentic Leonardo. Since she could never be shared or even acknowledged, each buyer would believe that he possessed the true Mona Lisa. The Mexican enterprise had been a virtual dry run—excellent training for their new and most remarkable coup.

"In selling that famous Murillo sometimes several times a week," the marqués explained to Decker, "I learned of that queer quirk in the brain of the collector that will cause him to buy what he can never sell again, what he can never exhibit and what will have to be kept hidden at all times."

3

A PERFECT CRIME, like a perfect cognac, should be swirled and savored, and with what Decker called "that strange quirk

* James H. Duveen, *Art Treasures and Intrigue.*

of vanity characteristic of the creative crook," the marqués recounted each step.

In the initial stage, Yves Chaudron became a habitué of the Louvre, his easel set up openly in the Salon Carré. Because of museum policy, he could not make his copy the same size as the original. Unfazed, Chaudron began a smaller replica of the Mona Lisa. He possessed exquisite dexterity as a forger, and his copy was exact in every detail. Enlarged slightly, it became his template.

While Chaudron painted in the Louvre, Valfierno traveled to Italy in search of an antique bed or armoire dating from around 1500. A headboard or the back panel of a chest, the wood seasoned by time and nature, was large enough to cut into six panels, measuring thirty-one-by-twenty-one-inches. Each would be a near-match to Leonardo's.

After purchasing an armoire of the required age and size and cutting the panels, the conspirators chopped up the remains and fed them to a fire in Chaudron's studio. He was upset because they had destroyed a beautiful antique, but Valfierno laughed and assured his friend that in a few months, he could buy another armoire—or a hundred more, each older and more beautiful.

In Paris, the marqués established luxurious headquarters on the Left Bank and stocked the place with cases of Chambertin, Roederer Cristal, and Napoleon Courvoisier. Fine wines, vintage champagne, and the smoothest cognac, served in Baccarat crystal, were necessary lubricants. While Valfierno prepared his seduction, Chaudron primed the panels to seal the wood. He undoubtedly followed the typical Renaissance procedure, first covering the bare wood with two successive layers of gesso and leaving it to dry. Depending on the weather, that would take at least two days. When the gesso dried, he applied a thick coating of white lead to form a binder between the panel and the paints. Without a binder, the wood would absorb the oil-based colors. When the panels dried, he went over each one with a pumice stone, sanding it until it was as smooth as a block of ice.

Often called "the second oldest profession," art forgery dates at least to the Roman Empire, when Athenian sculptors incised the signatures of Phidias and Praxiteles on their own inferior works, then sold them to their Roman conquerors as originals. The ancient Greeks never signed their sculpture, but the rubes from Rome did not know that. While forgery continued on a modest scale through the Renaissance when Ghiberti and Michelangelo created their own fake antiquities, the ancient profession reached pandemic levels only when American magnates entered the market. Renaissance paintings were the most speculative, the most desired, and the most frequently faked.

Forging is itself a fine art, and quality runs from crude imitation to near-flawless likeness. To fake the most famous face in art history was both daring and daunting. It required extraordinary precision and technical accuracy. A master like Chaudron would consult the best sources from Leonardo's time to learn which materials were available to him. Chaudron's bible would have been *Il Libro dell' Arte,* by Cennino Cennini. It was the authoritative source on the techniques and materials used by Renaissance and pre-Renaissance artists.

Chaudron would never make an obvious mistake, such as using cobalt blue, Chinese white, or cadmium yellow, paints popular in 1911 but not available in the 1500s. He would have mixed his own paints according to Renaissance formulas. Mona Lisa's true colors were probably never vivid, but they were clearer and brighter than the now muddy shades. Age, humidity, numerous varnishings, and botched conservation attempts had distorted Leonardo's palette, grays and greens turning to brown and blues to green. Chaudron had to compensate accordingly.

Although Leonardo's original colors can only be guessed, he probably used walnut oil as a base and had Verona green, lapis lazuli, red ocher, vermilion, and burnt umber on his palette. He may have added a trace of the vermilion directly to the white lead base coat to enhance Mona Lisa's skin tone. He also may have applied fine layers of burnt umber directly onto the undercoat to create shadows.

Color was only one of many challenges Mona Lisa presented to a forger. Leonardo did not mix his paints on a palette. He applied each one directly to the panel, painting the thinnest layers of color, one on top of the other, and achieving effects of great delicacy, blurring the edges particularly around the corners of the eyes and mouth. Mona Lisa is softly seductive, not an overtly provocative painted lady of the night, all hard edges and bold come-ons. She is ephemeral in her charms, perceived through the gentle play of shadow and light, and like a shadow, slipping away when you think your grasp is firm.

Blending color and glazes through multiple layers, so thin that they are almost translucent, gives Mona Lisa her unique aura. It creates the blurred *sfumato* effect, as if she is seen through a fine mist or a haze of smoke. Leonardo's brushstrokes are imperceptible, and his shades meld. Even in the landscape behind her, there are no distinct changes in color. The absence of defined edges to follow was a further test of Chaudron's skill.

Once the image was replicated, he had to force the paint to crack to mimic the fissures that mar the painting's surface. According to recent scientific studies, *craquelure* has various causes. That detailed technical information was not known in 1911, and Chaudron probably falsified the defect called premature *craquelure* caused by the way the artist layered the paint. If Chaudron applied a color with a low oil content over an oilier one, the upper layer of paint would dry before the under layer, causing the surface to crack. Or he might have created the *craquelure* with a needle, scratching a web of lines in the outer layer of varnish, then rubbing dirt into the cracks with a pad of cotton wool. Finally, a forger of Chaudron's quality would not neglect the back. Using a fine drill, he would simulate the damage caused by insects. Woodworms feast on old panel paintings, tunneling into the backs because they do not like paint.

No artist can reproduce every line, every shadow, and every dimension of a painting. There will always be small deviations that may not affect the general appearance but are undeniable. If the best forgery is placed beside the original, an expert may spot the differences. Further investigation would reveal the fraud. But Chaudron's Mona Lisas would never be seen with Leonardo's. That was the beauty of the game. Doubt was eliminated. No comparison would ever be made or even believed possible, because each buyer would be convinced that he possessed the one true da Vinci. It was more than a perfect crime, the marqués boasted; it was a service to mankind.

"I shall always contend that a forged painting so cleverly executed as to puzzle experts is as valuable an addition to the art wealth of the world as the original," he told Decker. "If the beauty is there in the picture, why cavil at the method by which it was obtained."

4

GIVEN THE COMPLEXITY of the enterprise, Chaudron painted quickly. When the paint dried on each new work, the marqués sailed to the States. To avoid arousing suspicion, he made six separate trips over the span of a year. On each crossing, he carried a new Mona Lisa in his Vuitton luggage. Reproductions of masterworks had become commonplace, and each time he declared his cargo and passed through New York customs without incident.

By early summer 1911, the sting was set. The six forgeries were stashed safely in a New York bank vault and ready for sale, each with a price tag roughly equivalent to $15 million today. The six sheep were lined up to be fleeced. Only one step remained. Mona Lisa had to vanish from the Louvre.

For this final detail, Valfierno needed someone with inside knowledge of the museum, and he recruited Vincenzo "Leonardo" Peruggia. Peruggia was an artisan, possessing precise knowledge and craft. Since he had been employed by the Louvre, he was both familiar with the museum and a familiar presence to the guards, and since he had built the glass box frame for Mona Lisa, he could remove the painting easily. He, in turn, recruited two accomplices, the Lancelotti brothers.

Valfierno had begun wooing Peruggia while he was working as a framer at the Louvre, and they rehearsed every detail of the operation numerous times over a period of weeks and months. The marqués provided a master key, a map of the museum, and more francs than Peruggia had ever imagined possessing in his lifetime—and that was only a first installment.

As Valfierno related the story, late in the afternoon of Sunday, August 20, the three men visited the Louvre. One of them carried a brown paper parcel tied with string and containing the uniform of museum workers, three starched, knee-length white smocks. They lingered in the Salon Carré. The crowds were thin, and the guard was drowsy. By the four o'clock closing hour, the three had disappeared.

As the museum emptied for the night, Peruggia led the men to a storage room between the Galerie d'Apollon and the Salle Duchâtel, where the copyists stored their supplies. Crouched in the darkness in the cramped closet, wedged among easels and paint boxes, the friends shared a hunk of cheese and a small flask of wine and waited for morning.

Because the Louvre was closed to the public on Mondays, the only people in the galleries would be maintenance men and security guards. Around six-thirty a.m., the museum workers began arriving. The three thieves, now dressed in the anonymous white smocks, mingled easily. The marqués relished the simplicity of their disguise.

"It was a psychological tour de force. Our success depended upon one thing—the fact that a workman in a white blouse in the Louvre is as free from suspicion as an unlaid egg."

He had mapped an exact route for the men to follow through the museum complex and out to the street. They would lift Mona Lisa from the wall and carry her through the Salon Carré into the Grande Galerie. There they would turn to the right and continue through to the Salle de Sept-Mètres, where the Italian primitives hung. In the right wall at the corner, a door led to a back stairway used only by museum employees. They would carry Mona Lisa down the stairs, unlock the door at the bottom, and go through to the Cour du Sphinx. Across the court was the Cour Visconti, where a door opened to the street. There they would remove their smocks and exit the museum.

The first stage proceeded flawlessly. The usual attendant did not come in, which left one guard to cover the Grande and Petite Galeries, the Salon Carré, and the Salon d'Apollon. When that guard took a cigarette break, Peruggia and his accomplices saw their opportunity.

Peruggia was a small man, and lifting Mona Lisa off the wall was not a simple feat for him. The wood panel with the frame and the glass box were cumbersome. With one of the Lancelottis serving as lookout, Peruggia and the other brother removed the painting. They passed unnoticed through the three empty galleries to the service stairway. On the small landing, Peruggia took a screwdriver from his pocket and, working quickly, unfastened the outer frame. Opening the glass box that he had constructed was easy, but taking the painting out of the ornate antique frame, the marqués said, "had them sweating." Packing paper—stuffed inside to hold the panel in place—ripped, leaving a paper trail across the landing.

Although it seemed an eternity, in five minutes, Mona Lisa was free. Pushing the two frames into a corner of the landing, Peruggia slid the painting under his smock and dashed down the stairs. The Lancelottis returned to the Salle de Sept-Mètres to keep watch. The operation was proceeding perfectly. "Then," the marqués confided, "for the first time our beautiful scheme failed to click." The door at the bottom of the staircase was locked, and the key he had given Peruggia did not fit. He blamed the Italian for being careless. Valfierno had repeatedly instructed Peruggia to go to the Louvre and test the key. The Italian had failed to carry out orders, and the escape route was blocked.

Valfierno's voice dropped dramatically. "Imagine. That one little lapse nearly ruined us."

Peruggia still had the screwdriver he had used to open the frames, and again he worked quickly. He had removed the brass doorknob and was starting on the lock when he heard his lookouts whistle. The coast was no longer clear.

Peruggia was sitting on the bottom steps in an attitude of annoyance, leaning lightly against Mona Lisa, who was behind his back, hidden under his smock, when the plumber Sauve padded down the stairs and became an unwitting accomplice. The instant Peruggia heard the footsteps behind him, he began cursing that some fool had locked the door. Sauve, using his master key and a pair of pliers, opened it. After that helpful deed, the rest was a cakewalk.

Telling Peruggia to leave the door ajar until the knob could be replaced, the plumber went on his merry way, and Mona Lisa went on hers. The brothers joined Peruggia, and together, they crossed the Cour du Sphinx and entered the Cour Visconti. The Porte Visconti entrance by the side of the Seine was unattended. The guard, who had been washing the vestibule, had gone for a fresh bucket of water and stopped on his way back to rest in the sun. The thieves could see him under a red umbrella, sleeping soundly. Taking off their smocks, they slipped out of the museum. By nine o'clock, Peruggia was hurrying along the Quai du Louvre, the Leonardo, wrapped in the white museum smock, in his arms and his accomplices on the lookout behind him.

The marqués swirled his cognac, savoring the bouquet and the memory.

"Everybody tried to make it easy for us. What helped us was as much dumbness as luck." Within the hour, Peruggia reported to the marqués's headquarters on the Left Bank. Valfierno said, "We gave ourselves up to a quality of hilarious enjoyment. The big job was finished, the great coup had been pulled off. The most magnificent single theft in the history of the world had been accomplished, and we were proud and happy."

Valfierno and Chaudron celebrated at a lavish dinner, wining and dining through the night. The American buyers had been told to read the newspaper on Tuesday, August 22. Although he had lined them up months before, the marqués had been cagey. He had left the transactions open—no palms crossed, no contracts sealed, no irrevocable commitments made until the identity of the art for sale was emblazoned on the front page of every newspaper in New York and Paris.

The triumphant pair waited for the first editions of the morning papers. They expected the missing Mona Lisa to fill the headlines. Instead, Paris greeted her disappearance with a stunning silence. There was no picture, no word. There wasn't even a white lie noting that she had been removed for cleaning.

Neither Valfierno nor Chaudron had gone anywhere near

the museum, not even venturing across the Seine for two days. They had perfect alibis for Sunday and Monday. Suspecting a double cross, they stormed to Peruggia's apartment and roused him rudely from his bed. At first, dazed and confused, then angry and defensive, Peruggia opened a closet, took out a white wooden box, unwrapped a red cloth, and there she was. Chaudron, stunned by the true art, picked up Mona Lisa and held her like a man transfixed. The marqués had imagined every possible scenario except the actual one. No one at the Louvre had noticed that Mona Lisa was missing.

He and Chaudron passed a second anxious day. That evening, *Le Temps* published an extra edition with the news, and on Wednesday, August 23, 1911, banner headlines in papers around the world announced that the unimaginable had occurred. A front-page article in *The New York Times* reported:

LA GIOCONDA IS STOLEN IN PARIS

MASTERPIECE OF LEONARDO DA VINCI

VANISHES FROM THE LOUVRE

Once the story broke, the sting moved swiftly. The marqués contacted each expectant buyer and arranged the deliveries. Reliving his greatest moment, he could not repress his delight.

"Chaudron almost died of joy and pride when he learned the prices his work had brought," he told Decker.

The forgeries sold quickly, netting the equivalent of $90 million, and the conspirators kept the prize. The partners left the true Leonardo hidden in Peruggia's apartment, divided the money, and disappeared from Paris. After so many successful years together, mastermind and forger went their separate ways. Yves Chaudron retired to a country château outside Paris, occasionally doing a little work to keep from growing rusty, and Valfierno moved on to the next opportunity.

"We would have returned the painting voluntarily to the Louvre in due time," he told Decker, "had not a minor member of the cast idiotically run away with it. To his elementary mind, it followed that the painting must be the prize."

The marqués dismissed the ensuing imbroglio as a farce caused by stupidity and greed. He never really cared what became of Mona Lisa as long as she remained lost for a reasonable time. She was much too hot to handle, he said, and any attempt to sell her would have meant immediate arrest. Even an obvious copy would have attracted attention. But Peruggia never understood that Mona Lisa herself was not for sale. Although he had been paid handsomely for his role, Peruggia gambled away the money on the Riviera and soon was looking for more. He had Mona Lisa secured in the false-bottomed case that he had built himself to her exact measurements, but he had no idea how to dispose of her until he saw Alfredo Geri's ad.

The muezzin was chanting the sunset call to prayer in the minaret of the mosque when Eduardo de Valfierno finished his story. The terrace had grown cold. The marqués drained the last drop of cognac and, with a farewell salute to the American, disappeared into the evening crowd of Arab shopkeepers, French Foreign Legionnaires, and Spanish dockworkers in Morocco's darkening alleys.

A PERFECT STORY

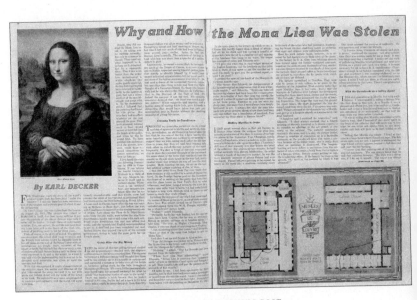

THE *SATURDAY EVENING POST*

The Karl Decker story featured in the June 25, 1932, issue of the *Saturday Evening Post* was a perfect story, but was it the true story?

(Courtesy of the General Research Division, The New York Public Library,

Astor, Lenox, and Tilden Foundations)

I

EIGHTEEN YEARS LATER, on June 25, 1932, Karl Decker broke the story. In an exclusive article in the *Saturday Evening Post* headlined WHY AND HOW THE MONA LISA WAS STOLEN, he revealed the confession of the late Marqués Eduardo de Valfierno. Decker's tale of a suave international scam artist executing a brilliant sting and then making his stunning confession is a romantic adventure, far more satisfying than Vincenzo Peruggia's quixotic myth.

It made a perfect story, but was it the true story?

Whether the Marqués Eduardo de Valfierno was a reliable source is certainly questionable. Whether he even existed is equally dubious. Since Decker never revealed the marqués's true name or offered any corroborating evidence, nothing can be verified.

As with Mona Lisa herself, very little is certain about the case. To separate indisputable facts from fancy: The person who removed Mona Lisa from her frames on Monday, August 21, 1911, in a back stairway of the Louvre Museum was Vincenzo Peruggia, the Italian-born glazier who had helped to build a glass-enclosed frame for the painting. There is no question that Peruggia performed the actual theft. He left his calling card. The left thumbprint on the frame was his, and examinations by French and Italian experts proved beyond a reasonable doubt that the Mona Lisa he returned was the same painting that he stole. Beyond that are only questions.

The long absence, the random recovery, and his spurious grasp of history cast doubt on Peruggia's claim that he alone planned and executed such a stunning crime. His account sounds dubious, and Decker's story sounds phony. If Peruggia was not the lone thief and the marqués and his expert forger were fictions, the mystery remains: Who masterminded the theft and, even more puzzling, why?

From the first, there were rumors of politics at play. The theft conveniently coincided with the flare-up in Morocco between France and Germany. Was Mona Lisa stolen to avert or foment war? To embarrass France? To rile Germany? There were persistent stories of a German man of means and middle age, a frequent visitor to the Louvre, who cultivated one of the Italian workers. He supposedly filled the young man's mind with false history and patriotic fervor. Over months of clever goading and suggestion, the German planted the notion that returning Mona Lisa to Italy would be a grand act of patriotism that would bring honor to the young man's family.

While the young Italian presumably was Peruggia, no trace of the German svengali has turned up. His motive remains obscure, and in any case, the denouement was a fizzle. The only trail left to follow is Decker's own.

2

SINCE HIS DAYS as a cub reporter for Hearst, Karl Decker had been making or manufacturing the news. He did not invent a story out of whole cloth, but embroidery and embellishment were journalistic skills he had learned from the master. The young reporter played by Hearst's rules, which meant pretty much anything goes to get or manufacture a story.

The motto "While others talk, the *Journal* acts" expressed the Hearst creed. If governments failed to right public wrongs, journalists should charge into the breach. In the 1890s, Hearst adopted the cause of Cuban rebels seeking independence from Spain. As his newspapers played the story, ruthless Spanish villains were denying the rights of Cuban freedom fighters, who were all noble and pure of heart. In his drumbeat to the Spanish-American War, Hearst dispatched the artist Frederic Remington to Havana to cover the impending conflict. According to a now classic account, finding the city calm, Remington telegraphed the publisher: EVERYTHING QUIET STOP THERE WILL BE NO WAR STOP COMING HOME. Hearst wired back: PLEASE REMAIN STOP YOU FURNISH PICTURES STOP I WILL FURNISH WAR.

At the height of his Cuba campaign, Hearst seized on the plight of a damsel in distress. Evangelina Cisneros, daughter of a revolutionary family, was nineteen, beautiful, and imprisoned in Havana. Hearst made her cause a crusade. He sent the young Karl Decker to spring Evangelina from her jail cell. Decker rented a house across an alley from the prison. One midnight after her prison bars were filed and the guards bribed, he laid a ladder across the rooftops, climbed to the jail, and spirited Evangelina away.

In the purple prose of Nathaniel Hawthorne's son, Julian, who was on the Hearst payroll, the rescue had the elements of a classic myth: "A tropic island, embosomed in azure seas off the coast of the Spanish Main, a cruel war waged by the minions of despotism against the spirit of patriotism and liberty, a beautiful maiden risking all for her country, captured, insulted, persecuted, and cast into a loathsome dungeon," and her savior, "a young American of the best and oldest strain, with the Constitution in his backbone and the Declaration of Independence in his eyes."

Decker and Evangelina arrived in New York to front-page headlines and a hero's welcome. A tumultuous crowd of more than one hundred thousand cheered them at a rally in Madison Square Garden. Their next stop was Washington, where President William McKinley received them at the White House and praised Decker's exploit as "a heroic deed." A few days later, the U.S.S. *Maine* exploded in the harbor of Havana, either from spontaneous internal combustion or from a mine explosion. The cause was never determined, but "Remember the *Maine*" became a rallying cry that drew the United States into war.

In its daring and in its complete disregard for international law, the Cisneros jailbreak is unsurpassed in the often tawdry and tarnished annals of American journalism. Decker became the poster boy for the "journalism of action." His name continued to make headlines in the Hearst papers:

JOURNAL PLANNED TO CONDUCT
MILITARY EXPEDITION TO CUBA
HEADED BY KARL DECKER

SPAIN MAKES WAR ON *JOURNAL,*
SEIZING THE YACHT *BUCCANEER*
TO ARREST KARL DECKER WHO WAS BELIEVED
TO BE ABOARD

SPAIN FEARS *JOURNAL* AND KARL DECKER

3

DECKER'S MOST RELIABLE SOURCE was often himself. As Julian Hawthorne wrote, "He had imagination to conceive, ingenuity to plan, coolness and resolution to carry out, and then—best of all—that wonderful power of belief in the possibility of the impossible."

Decker loved a big story, and in January 1914, there was no bigger story than the recovery of the lost Leonardo. Through the years, he must have followed her misadventures and recognized the tantalizing tease waiting to be woven into a fiction as remarkable as Mona Lisa herself.

Maybe he was simply in the right place at the right time for an exclusive story. The possibility is no more or less plausible than anything else about the Mona Lisa caper. On the other hand, Decker may not have been in Casablanca at all. There are no stories datelined Morocco with his byline in the *New York Journal* of January 1914, and the gentleman thief Marqués Eduardo de Valfierno reads like a stock character. That the two men happened to meet on the day the missing Mona Lisa returned to the Louvre seems more than serendipity. That Decker had the scoop on the criminal case holding the attention of the world and sat on the story for more than twenty years seems highly improbable.

When the *Saturday Evening Post* story broke, both the heist and the marqués had passed into history. Decker was sixty-four. His feats of derring-do were old news, and the style of heroic journalism that had made him a legend was discredited. By the 1930s, American journalism had undergone a bleaching. *The New York Times*'s staid style, the antithesis of Hearst's yellow journalism, had become the model. Readers were better educated and less easily gulled. The new reporter was a cool observer transcribing from the sidelines, not plunging headlong into a story. "Just the facts, please" became the motto.

For Decker, the *Saturday Evening Post* article might have been a chance to make headlines again and reinvigorate a waning career. He wrote it in the old sensational style that he had mastered in his youth and that can be embarrassing to read today: "For twenty-one years, the story of the world's single greatest theft has been kept 'under the smother.' Until now there has been not even a hint of the tangled and intricate plot. . . ."

A case can be made that, with his glory days behind him, Karl Decker played fast and loose with the truth, lifting elements of his story directly from various Paris newspapers and weaving them into a more memorable, more satisfying scenario than Peruggia's confession. The Marqués de Valfierno's description of how the heist was carried out corresponds to the report made by Magistrate Henri Drioux and contradicts Peruggia's sworn testimony. The notion of a sting was suggested in the days immediately following the theft by Joseph Reinach of *les Amis du Louvre* and published in *Le Temps*.

If Decker spiced the story, he left a few clues. One is the forger's name. *Chaudron* means a large kettle or cauldron, something the French might use to prepare a cassoulet. Decker's *Saturday Evening Post* article seems to be a *chaudron* in which he has mixed bits of evidence and conjecture, laced with generous pinches of invention, imagination, and wry humor. There is also a street in Paris, Rue Chaudron, located just a couple of blocks from the apartment where Mona Lisa remained hidden for two years.

In perhaps another entertaining flourish, the forger allegedly honed his craft by faking the works of Bartolomé Murillo, whose favorite subject was the Immaculate Conception. Decker's article was an immaculate conception of sorts. He provides no supporting material. Nothing in the article suggests that he ever interviewed Peruggia, who had been dead more than six years when the article appeared.

When Decker's exposé ran in the *Saturday Evening Post,* the *Los Angeles Times* called it "the most plausible explanation yet given of the strange theft from the Louvre of the Mona Lisa." The article went on, "Whether this story is authentic or the product of a lively imagination (not, of course, the author's but he may have been imposed upon) would be difficult to check without a great deal more data than are given in the *Post* account, but it is a fine, romantic tale, which ought to be true if it isn't."

Karl Decker's trail is as cold as everything else about the case. He died intestate in New York City in 1941 and was cremated. He left no family or heirs except his wife, Maude, who was then living alone and in failing health in a small walk-up apartment without a telephone on West Seventy-fifth Street.

In the mid-1940s, the novelist James M. Cain wanted to write a movie based on the *Post* article. He spent several years trying to track down information on Decker to acquire the rights, but he came up empty-handed. None of the magazines that had published Decker could help him, and his efforts to contact Maude Decker were unsuccessful.

Whether fact or fiction, the Marqués Eduardo de Valfierno was buried with Karl Decker. Only his alter ego lives on. Although he may have been nothing more than the kettle in which a reporter brewed a fanciful tale, today every list of history's legendary forgers includes the name Yves Chaudron.

THE PRISONER

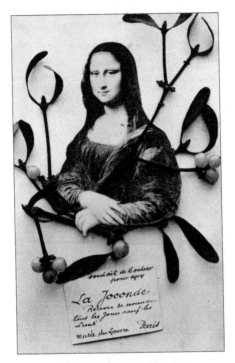

MONA LISA'S CALLING CARD

When Mona Lisa returned to the Louvre in
January 1914, the museum printed this calling
card, saying that Mona Lisa would once again
be receiving visitors every day except Monday.

(Courtesy of Roger-Viollet/Getty Images)

I

BEFORE AUGUST 21, 1911, Mona Lisa belonged to the realm of high art. After August 21, she became a staple of consumer culture. The pure beauty that François I made his own, that Leonardo clung to and Raphael copied, that Louis XIV and Napoleon took into their bedrooms became fair game for advertisers, authors, pop stars, and promoters.

Mona Lisa was spoofed for the first time in 1887, when she was pictured smoking a pipe. Since then many artists have parodied her or paid her homage, including Dalí, Léger, Marisol, Rauschenberg, and Peter Max. Duchamp painted a beard and mustache on a cheap postcard reproduction of Mona Lisa and added the inscription LHOOQ (*Elle a chaud au cul,* She has a hot ass). Andy Warhol silk-screened multiple Mona Lisa images, giving her the media status of Marilyn Monroe and Jackie O.

Nat King Cole, Bob Dylan, Elton John, Willie Nelson, even Britney Spears and hip-hop singer Slick Rick have sung about her. She has been fodder for science fiction and suspense writers from Ray Bradbury to Dan Brown, *Star Trek* to *Doctor Who.* Julia Roberts starred in *Mona Lisa Smile.* Looney Tunes made her a cartoon in *Louvre Come Back to Me,* and the Simpsons reduced her to a homophone, "Moanin' Lisa."

As the first mass masterpiece, she is a commodity like the Campbell Soup can. Insert a celebrity face over hers, and an instant ad or magazine cover is created. Jackie Kennedy,

Golda Meir, Monica Lewinsky, Joseph Stalin, and Salvador Dalí have all been Mona Lisa-ed.

Yet her mystery persists. Sigmund Freud went off on a flight of psychoanalytic fancy to understand and interpret her. He theorized: "Leonardo was fascinated by the smile of Mona Lisa because it had awakened something in him which had slumbered in his soul for a long time, in all probability an old memory." He suggested that Leonardo's "mother possessed that mysterious smile which he lost and which fascinated him so much when he found it again in the Florentine lady."

Others have read her smile as an expression of sweet perfidy, androgynous beauty, and desperate hope. It has been called "a deceitful mask," "a veiled threat," and the smirk of "a woman who has just dined off her husband."*

Although the truth could be as simple as aesthetic necessity—given the quality of dental hygiene in the 1500s, full smiles were far from comely—comparisons are made to "the strange smile of benign comprehension" that the Buddha wears, the "archaic smile" that animated ancient Grecian sculpture, and the Renaissance smile of Donatello's *David*.

In recent years, a pair of researchers in Holland studied Mona Lisa's smile using an emotion-recognition software program. The face-tracking technology read Mona Lisa's expression as 83 percent happy, 9 percent disgusted, 6 percent fearful, 2 percent angry, and less than 1 percent neutral. No wonder she is inscrutable.

Neurologists have analyzed her smile as the response of cranial nerve VII, which controls the facial muscles. According to studies made by a professor at Harvard University, Mona Lisa's smile appears and disappears depending on whether we

* Lawrence Durrell, *Justine.*

gaze at her peripherally or directly, which may explain why she seems to catch us looking at her.

The more that is said about her, the less seems certain. Every fresh study provokes more conjecture. One theory reduces her to a mathematical equation. The golden ratio and the significance of pi in Leonardo's work are the subject of earnest articles. Another theory alleges that Mona Lisa is a symbol of the Egyptian goddess Isis and encrypted in her image is the ancient secret of the Giza Pyramids. A computer scientist, juxtaposing Mona Lisa with Leonardo's self-portrait, surmises that she is the artist in drag.

There are even more exotic interpretations. Squinting at Mona Lisa reveals an infinity of hidden faces behind the famous mask, one devotee claims. Squint some more and a human skull metamorphoses behind her left shoulder. Cover the left side of your face and she appears confident; cover the right side and she seems reticent. Gaze at her by candlelight while blinking rapidly and her smile changes, her face assumes different expressions. A Japanese forensics expert believes that by analyzing Mona Lisa's skeletal structure, he can accurately re-create her voice, which, he says, has a low register for a woman.

2

ON DECEMBER 14, 1962, forty-nine years to the day after she began her Italian tour, Mona Lisa went on the road again. Curators were afraid to let her leave the Louvre a second time, but General Charles de Gaulle was the president of France and André Malraux was his minister of culture. They were a formidable pair, both masters at generating publicity.

With a $100-million insurance policy (approximately $608 million today), Mona Lisa sailed for the United States on the S.S. *France*. A police escort brought her to Le Havre, where the ship's captain was waiting on deck to welcome her. She had her own first-class cabin, with security guards in the cabin on one side and nervous Louvre curators and conservators in the cabin on the other. Outfitted in a custom-made 352-pound airtight, floatable, temperature-and-humidity-controlled container, constructed of steel alloy and padded with Styrofoam, she was the safest passenger on board the luxury liner.

When she arrived in New York, the director of the National Gallery, John Walker, was waiting at the dock with a Secret Service contingent. They transported her to Washington in a modified ambulance padded with foam rubber. All traffic was blocked from entering the Holland and Baltimore Harbor tunnels when she rode through. Because any change from the conditions that Mona Lisa was accustomed to might damage her irrevocably, Walker modified the air-conditioning system in the National Gallery so that "the atmosphere of her temporary home simulated the very air she had breathed in Paris."*

Mona Lisa had come a long way from her days in Vincenzo Peruggia's closet. Her American visit occurred at a low point in U.S.-French relations. Against American wishes, de Gaulle was going outside of NATO to arm France. Nevertheless, President Kennedy welcomed the illustrious visitor with the honors usually reserved for a head of state. The guest list for her white-tie reception included the Supreme Court justices, the governor of every state, both houses of Congress, and the full diplomatic corps.

When the National Gallery opened to the public, the line of visitors stretched down the Mall. Director Walker estimated that she was seen by more people "than had ever attended a

* John Walker, *Self Portrait with Donors.*

football game, a prize fight, or a World Series. . . . Her visit caused an esthetic explosion in the minds of many of those who saw her. . . . This great painting started some impulse toward beauty in human beings who had never felt that impulse before." After her Washington performance, Mona Lisa moved to the Metropolitan Museum in New York for another sold-out month-long engagement.

In 1974 she went on the road again. Mona Lisa flew for the first time, from Paris to Tokyo. To avoid any change in pressure during the flights, her aluminum travel case was fitted in a protective steel container. So many Japanese wanted to see her that each person was limited to a ten-second glimpse. Mona Lisa even had her own phone. Anyone in Japan could dial a special number, and she would answer, "Hi, my name is Lisa and I am known as the *Gioconda.*" From Tokyo, she went on to Moscow, where she was lionized again.

3

MONA LISA DOESN'T get around much anymore. France now has a law forbidding her from leaving the country. But six million people visit the Louvre each year, and it is safe to bet that just about every one of them stops in to see her. She has moved from her old spot in the Salon Carré to her own personal room in the Louvre, constructed at a price tag of $6.2 million and paid for by a Japanese television company. It is a virtual bunker.

Mona Lisa is set in concrete behind two sheets of bulletproof triple-laminated, nonreflective glass, separated by nine and a half inches (twenty-five centimeters). Her own personal bodyguards protect her from a repeat of 1911. In her new home, climatic conditions are constantly monitored. Ultrasound equipment and silica gel inside the display case keep her comfortable at all times, maintaining her temperature at a constant 55 degrees Fahrenheit with 50 percent humidity. The space between the sheets of glass creates a thermal buffer that prevents the fluctuating temperature of the room from affecting the temperature inside the case.

Once a year, Mona Lisa has a full checkup. In 1956 she was attacked twice—first with acid and then with a rock that was hurled through her protective glass, chipping her elbow. Like all old panel paintings, there are insect holes on her backside, but given her age, her adventures, and her popularity, she is in remarkably good shape. Her checkup is always scheduled in the spring, when the museum heating system is turned off and the outside temperature approximates her ideal levels of heat and humidity. A dozen curators, restoration and lab technicians, and some fifteen maintenance staff take part in the annual examination. Mona Lisa is removed from her display case and measured to see if her wood has expanded or contracted. While she is undressed, her display case is cleaned, and the silica gel is changed. She requires about twenty-six pounds of gel, which fill two oblong trays in the bottom of her case to regulate the moisture level.

The lady who sat stuffed in the false bottom of a valise in a tenement apartment for two years is coddled and cosseted more than any queen. She has undergone virtually every test that technology has devised—radiography, emissiography, and many types of imaging: multispectral, microtopographical, high-resolution three-dimensional, and infrared.

With all the tools of our high-tech age, Mona Lisa cannot be fathomed easily. She retains her unique power to drive otherwise rational men to unalloyed adoration, bitter denunciation, absurd conjecture, and audacious crime. Half a millennium after Leonardo painted her, Mona Lisa remains as she was to Baudelaire, a "mirror deep and dark." Revered and reviled in equal measure, subjected to adulation and insult, she performs a remarkable feat, bridging the divide between high and low culture. She has been derided as a femme fatale, an art fetish, and the queen of kitsch, and she goes on smiling, a picture of contained serenity, her mysteries intact, her secrets secure.

While she is art history's most enduring enigma, celebrity and mass communication have made her a tragic figure. After her theft, Mona Lisa was recovered physically but never spiritually. She was found and lost. Today Mona Lisa is seen by millions, yet unseen. For her own protection, "the most subtle homage that genius can pay to a human face" can never be contemplated again in a true light, free of the barricades.

Away from the hordes of tourists and digital cameras, out of the display case and "in the flesh," seen not in virtual reality but in the true reality of the painted panel, Mona Lisa enters the soul. This is the genius of Leonardo, lost since the theft created the icon.

Behind her impenetrable bulletproof glass, in her multimillion-dollar digs in a hall once called the Salle des États, she hangs in splendid isolation, alone except for François I, across the room in the *Wedding Feast at Cana.* It is bemusing and comforting to know that when the last camera has flashed and the last ogler has turned away, when the Louvre alarms are blinking and night falls over the mansard roofs of Paris, François is still keeping a possessive eye on his Mona Lisa.

ACKNOWLEDGMENTS

IN PURSUING Mona's Lisa's mysterious theft, I have been aided and abetted in many ways by many people. My valiant daughter, Francesca Chigounis, read, and reread, and reread the manuscript as if each time were a pleasure, not a penance, and with each reading, raised key questions and offered keen advice. My dauntless agent, F. Joseph Spieler, was a miracle worker at the outset, an unfailing source of encouragement and faith through the long slog, and a painstaking editor in the stretch. My astute and patient editor, Dan Frank, pushed me, kicking and screaming, to coherence. My thanks, also, to Doug Steel for his photographic wizardry, design skill, and abiding friendship; to Fran Bigman for steering the book through each step of the editorial process; to Maria Scotti Chapin, born on August 21, for leaving no word unchecked; to Evans Chigounis for tea and choice words; and to Wayne Furman and the Frederick Lewis Allen Room of the New York Public Library, my second home.

NOTES

Much of the information here is drawn from newspaper and magazine articles related to the theft and to the reports of the police investigation. I am also indebted to the fine authors who have gone before me, particularly. Jérôme Coignard, Milton Esterow, Fernande Olivier, Charles Nicholl, Roy McMullen, and John Richardson.

THE VANISHING ACT ·

9 AN ELEGANT LATIN AMERICAN "MARQUÉS": Information on the Marqués Eduard de Valfierno comes from Karl Decker, "How and Why the *Mona Lisa* Was Stolen," *Saturday Evening Post,* June 25, 1932.

25 PARIS WAS THE HUB FOR NEWS: Robert Desmond's *Information Process* and *Windows on the World.*

THE HUNT

34 THE FIRST TO FACE JUDGE DRIOUX: Jérôme Coignard's *On a Volé la Joconde.*

48 THE BOND STREET SHOWROOM OF DUVEEN BROTHERS: James H. Duveen, *Art Treasures and Intrigue.*

49 A THIRD CLANDESTINE PARTNER: Joseph Duveen wrote of Bernard Berenson: "I advise caution as all are agreed that he will never play the second fiddle but must lead the band, if not conduct it. It could be dangerous to be out of step with him."

51 *CHERCHEZ L'AMÉRICAIN:* Frederick Lewis Allen, *The Great Pierpont Morgan.*

THE BLANK WALL

65 THE RISE OF A POPULAR PRESS: Robert Desmond's *Information Process* and *Windows on the World.*

70 THE FACES OF THE CROWDS WERE CHANGING: Henry T. Peck, *The New Baedeker 1856-1914, Being Casual Notes of an Irresponsible Traveler.*

70 THE GRAND TOUR: Elizabeth I originated the idea of sending the young English lords who would inherit the realm on a "grand tour" of the Continent to acquire culture. Dr. Johnson was generally opposed to the practice, with one pragmatic exception: "Indeed, if a young man is wild and must run after women and bad company, it is better this should be done abroad, as, on his return, he can break off such connections and begin at home a new man."

72 A THIEF BRINGS US A STATUE: On the articles from the *Paris-Journal* and *Le Matin* in this section and the next, I have relied for the most part on the translations of Milton Esterow in *The Art Stealers.*

NOT THE USUAL SUSPECTS

85 "WE HAVE INFECTED THE PICTURES": Pablo Picasso, *Picasso on Art.*

87 BORN AMÉLIE LANG: Fernande Olivier, *Loving Picasso.*

89 "YOU COULD OWE MONEY FOR YEARS": Picasso, *Picasso on Art.*

89 LEO AND GERTRUDE STEIN: James R. Mellow's *Charmed Circle,* and Roger Shattuck's *The Banquet Years.*

90 APOLLINAIRE GREW INCREASINGLY ALARMED: Fernande Olivier, *Picasso and His Friends.*

93 WHILE AWAITING MONA LISA: Milton Esterow, *The Art Stealers.*

94 APOLLINAIRE WAS UNDER ARREST: Francis Steegmuller, *Guillaume Apollinaire, Poet Among the Painters.*

98 THE LOUVRE THIEF: Since Honoré Joseph Géry Pieret was called variously Géry and Pieret, I refer to him as Géry for consistency.

100 THE POET IN HANDCUFFS: Esterow, *The Art Stealers.*

102 THE STUDIO PRESENTED A SCENE: Olivier, *Picasso and His Friends.*

106 APOLLINAIRE WOULD RECALL SOMETIME LATER: Apollinaire, *Apollinaire par lui-même.*

106 FERNANDE GAVE A DIFFERENT VERSION: Olivier, *Picasso and His Friends.*

112 YEARS LATER, WHEN IT WAS SAFE: Picasso, *Picasso on Art.*

112 FERNANDE PINPOINTED THE FATAL FLAW: Olivier, *Picasso and His Friends.*

114 ON THE 31ST DAY OF AUGUST: Guillaume Apollinaire, *Selected Poems.*

115 ANDRÉ BILLY, A WRITER: André Billy, *Avec Apollinaire, Souvenirs Inédits.*

THE MYSTERY WOMAN

126 BY 1503, ARTISTS WERE FLOCKING TO ROME: During Julius II's papacy (1503–1513), he commissioned Michelangelo to sculpt a papal tomb (1505) and to paint the Sistine Chapel ceiling (1508), Bramante to build St. Peter's (1505), and Raphael to fresco the *Stanze* (1508).

128 SHE IS A STRANGE PAINTING: Mona Lisa is variously interpreted as a reflection on man and nature, the one immortal, the other transitory, or a cosmic meditation. Leonardo saw the individual as a microcosmos and the elements of one as a metaphor for the other. The human skeleton corresponds to the earth and the pumping blood to moving water. The passions are fire, and the soul is the wind.

129 FINANCIAL RECORDS SUGGEST: Charles Nicholl, *Leonardo da Vinci: Flights of the Mind.*

131 IN HIS NOTES ON PAINTING: *Leonardo on Painting.*

132 BY PURE COINCIDENCE: A Frenchman, probably the historian Jules Michelet, was the first to suggest the love affair. Michelet wrote that Mona Lisa was so seductive, even Leonardo—"the complete man, balanced, all-powerful in all things, who summarized all the past, anticipated the future . . . was taken in by the snare. . . ." Jules Verne, as a young man and something of a naïf, composed a play about the illusory romance, and the Italian Romantic poet Enrico Panzacchi celebrated it in verse. He imagined Lisa's husband refusing to accept the portrait when he saw the smile on his wife's lips. Suspecting the worst, he returned the painting to the artist. We don't know what he did with his wife.

> *Messer Francesco suo sposo e signore*
> *Tornato vide l'opra e il mutamento*
> *Fece col capo un segno di scontento*
> *E il ritatto rimase as suo pittore.*

> *Signore Francesco her husband and lord*
> *Came back to view the work and seeing the change in his wife*
> *Shook his head in disgust*
> *And returned the painting to the painter.*

132 TODAY WE KNOW: Mohen et al., Mona Lisa: *Inside the Painting.*

135 ACCORDING TO CELLINI: Benvenuto Cellini's autobiography.

139 IN A VALIANT EFFORT AT RECONCILIATION: Nicholl, *Leonardo da Vinci.*

139 LISA DEL GIOCONDO: Giuseppe Pallanti, Mona Lisa *Revealed: The True Identity of Leonardo's Model.*

140 IN LEONARDO'S LAST WILL AND TESTAMENT: Janice Shell and Grazioso Sironi, "Salai and Leonardo's Legacy," *The Burlington Magazine* 133, no. 1055 (February 1991).

145 IN THE EIGHTEENTH CENTURY: André Felibien, *Entretiens sur les vies et sur les ouvrages des plus excellents peintres anciens et modernes.* Paris: Societé d'édition "Les Belles Lettres," 1987.

146 TO FLAUNT THE SUPERIORITY: The structural condition of the Louvre was so bad that it closed again in 1796. It reopened fully on July 14, 1801.

151 A BRITISH GALAHAD: Walter Pater, *Renaissance: Studies in Art and Poetry.*

153 INVESTIGATORS HAD CHASED TIPS: René Casselari, *Dramas of French Crime.*

A LETTER FROM LEONARDO

166 ALPHONSE BERTILLON WAS DYING: When he died, Bertillon was working on a plan to make future art fraud impossible. A few days before his death, he said: "Every artist will, in the future, place his thumb or any finger he may desire on the moist pigment together with his signature. He will make a duplicate of the impression on the usually prepared paper, which will be deposited with the École des Beaux-Arts. This paper will be photographed and the copies made kept on hand for distribution among collectors and dealers as the occasion may demand." Quoted in *The New York Times,* Feb. 13, 1914.

183 HENRY DUVEEN HAD TOLD A VERY DIFFERENT STORY: Duveen, *Art Treasures and Intrigue.*

THE STING

191 NEW YEAR'S 1914: Karl Decker, "How and Why the *Mona Lisa* Was Stolen," *Saturday Evening Post,* June 25, 1932.

199 FORGING IS ITSELF A FINE ART: Frank Arnau, *The Art of the Faker.*

A PERFECT STORY

217 THE NOVELIST JAMES M. CAIN: The papers of James M. Cain are in the Library of Congress.

THE PRISONER

221 SINCE THEN MANY ARTISTS: Roy McMullen, Mona Lisa: *Picture and Myth;* see also the Web site, www.monalisamania.com.

225 SHE HAS MOVED FROM HER OLD SPOT: McMullen, Mona Lisa.

BIBLIOGRAPHY

PERIODICALS

Architectural Review, May 1910
Art Bulletin, September 1941, December 1977, June 1985
Art News, September 1991
Atlantic Monthly, March 1929
Art and Antiques, January 1987 digital self-portrait
Art News, 1907–1912, 1991, 1992
Bookman, November 1911
Burlington Magazine, September 1947, March 1973
Gazette des Beaux Arts, November 1989, March 1993
Journal of Forensic Sciences, November 1992
Journal of the History of Ideas, April 1940, April 1956
Modern Language Review V, 74, 1979
Saturday Evening Post, June 1932
Smithsonian, May 1999
Urban History, August 2006

NEWSPAPERS

Chicago Tribune
Le Figaro
Le Matin
L'Illustration
London *Times*
Paris-Journal
Le Temps
Los Angeles Times
New York Journal
Paris Herald

BIBLIOGRAPHY

The New York Times
The Washington Post

BOOKS

Alexander, Edward P. *Museums in Motion.* Nashville: American Association for State and Local History, 1979.

Allen, Frederick Lewis. *The Great Pierpont Morgan.* New York: Harper, 1949.

Andersen, Wayne. *Picasso's Brothel.* New York: Other Press, 2004.

Apollinaire, Guillaume. *The Poet Assassinated and Other Stories,* trans. Ron Padgett. San Francisco: North Point Press, 1984.

——. *Selected Poems,* trans. Oliver Bernard. Anvil Press Poetry, 2003.

Arnau, Frank. *The Art of the Faker: 3,000 Years of Deception,* trans. Maxwell Brownjohn. Boston: Little, Brown, 1961.

Baedeker, Karl. *Paris and Its Environs 1910.* New York: Charles Scribner's Sons, 1910.

Berger, Robert. *Public Access to Art in Paris.* University Park, Pa.: Pennsylvania State University Press, 1999.

Belting Hans. *Invisible Masterpiece,* trans. Helen Atkins. Chicago: University of Chicago Press, 2000.

Bertillon, Alphonse. *Alphonse Bertillon's Instructions,* trans. Gallus Muller. New York: AMS Press, 1975.

Billy, André. *Avec Apollinaire, Souvenirs Inédits.* Paris: La Palatine, 1966.

Bramly, Serge. *Mona Lisa,* trans. Alexandra Campbell. London: Thames and Hudson, 1996.

Cabanne, Pierre. *Picasso: Life and Time,* trans. Harold J. Salemson. New York: Morrow, 1977.

Cahanne, Pierre. *The Great Collectors.* New York: Farrar, Straus, 1963.

Campbell, Gordon. *Renaissance Art and Architecture.* New York: Oxford University Press, 2004.

Casselari, Rene. *Dramas of French Crime.* London: Hutchinson & Co., 1920.

Clark, Kenneth. *Leonardo da Vinci.* London: Viking, 1988.

Cocteau, Jean. *Souvenir Portraits,* trans. Jesse Browner. New York: Paragon House, 1990.

Coignard, Jérôme. *On a Volé la Joconde.* Paris: A. Biro, 1990.

De Beatis, Antonio. *Travel Journal of Antonio de Beatis,* trans. R. Hale and J.M.A. Lindon. London: Hakluyt Society, 1979.

Decker, Karl. *The Story of Evangelina Cisneros.* New York: Continental Publishing Co., 1898.

Desmond, Robert. *The Information Process.* Iowa City: University of Iowa Press, 1977.

———. *Windows on the World.* Iowa City: University of Iowa Press, 1980.

Duveen, James H. *Art Treasures and Intrigue.* Garden City, N.Y.: Doubleday, Doran & Company, 1935.

Elderfield, John. *Picasso's Brothel.* New York: Other Press, 2002.

Esterow, Milton. *The Art Stealers.* New York: Macmillan, 1973.

Franck, Dan. *Bohemians: The Birth of Modern Art, Paris 1900–1930.* London: Weidenfeld & Nicolson, 2001.

Freud, Sigmund. *Leonardo da Vinci: A Study in Psychosexuality,* trans. A. A. Brill. New York: Random House, 1947.

Gayford, Martin, and Karen Wright, eds. *The Grove Book of Art Writing.* New York: Grove Press, 2000.

Gombrich, Ernst Hans. *Art and Illusion.* New York: Pantheon Books, 1961.

Green, Christopher, ed. *Picasso's* Les Demoiselles d'Avignon. New York: Cambridge University Press, 2001.

Heywood, Ian. *Faking It.* Brighton, England: Harvester Press, 1987.

Hibbert, Christopher. *The Grand Tour.* London: Weidenfeld & Nicolson, 1969.

Hudsen, Kenneth. *A Social History of Museums.* Atlantic Highlands, N.J.: Humanities Press, 1975.

Jacobs, Fredrika. *Living Image in Renaissance Art.* New York: Cambridge University Press, 2005.

Janouch, Gustav. *Conversations with Kafka,* trans. Goronwy Rees. London: Derek Verschoyle, 1953.

Jones, Mark, ed. *Fake?: The Art of Deception.* Berkeley: University of California Press, 1990.

Kafka, Franz. *Diaries 1910–1923,* ed. Max Brod. New York: Alfred A. Knopf, 1988.

Kemp, Martin. *Leonardo da Vinci.* New York: Oxford University Press, 2007.

Leader, Darian. *Stealing the* Mona Lisa. New York: Counterpoint, 2002.

Lebovics, Herbert. Mona Lisa's *Escort: André Malraux and the Reinvention of French Culture.* Ithaca, N.Y.: Cornell University Press, 1999.

Leech, Carolyn Apperson. *When Mona Lisa Came Home, Florence, December 1913.* Chicago: Alderbrink Press, 1914.

Leitch, David. *Discriminating Thief.* New York: Holt, Rinehart and Winston, 1969.

Leonardo da Vinci. *The Complete Works.* Cincinnati, Ohio: David & Charles, 2006.

Leonardo da Vinci. *Notebooks,* trans. Edward McCurdy. New York: Empire State Book Company, 1923.

Leonardo da Vinci. *Leonardo on Painting,* ed. Martin Kemp. New Haven: Yale University Press, 1989.

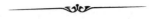
Livingston, Margaret. *Vision and Art*. New York: Harry N. Abrams, 2002.

Lucas, E. V. *A Wanderer in Paris*. New York: Macmillan, 1913.

Mailer, Norman. *Portrait of Picasso as a Young Man*. New York: Atlantic Monthly Press, 1995.

MacGregor-Hastie, Roy. *Picasso's Women*. London: Oberon, 1999.

Malraux, André. *Picasso's Mask*. New York: Holt, Rinehart & Winston, 1976.

McClellan, Andrew. *Inventing the Louvre*. New York: Cambridge University Press, 1994.

McLean, Hugh. *Rogues in the Gallery*. Boston: David R. Godine, 1981.

McMullen, Roy. Mona Lisa: *Picture and Myth*. Boston: Houghton Mifflin, 1975.

Mellow, James R. *Charmed Circle: Gertrude Stein & Company*. New York: Praeger, 1974.

Meyer, Karl Ernst. *The Plundered Past*. New York: Atheneum, 1973.

Mohen, Jean-Pierre, Menu, Michel, and Mottin, Bruno. Mona Lisa: *Inside the Painting*. New York: Abrams, 2006.

Nicholl, Charles. *Leonardo da Vinci: Flights of the Mind*. New York: Penguin, 2005.

O'Connor, Harvey. *Mellon's Millions*. New York: John Day Company, 1933.

Olivier, Fernande. *Loving Picasso*, trans. Christine Baker. New York: Abrams, 2001.

———. *Picasso and His Friends*, trans. Jane Miller. London: Heinemann, 1964.

———. *Souvenirs Intimes*. Paris: Calmann-Lévy, 1988.

Paglia, Camille. *Sexual Personae*. New Haven: Yale University Press, 1990.

Pallanti, Giuseppe. Mona Lisa *Revealed: The True Identity of Leonardo's Model*, trans. Timothy Stroud. Milan: SKIRA, 2006.

Pater, Walter. *Renaissance: Studies in Art and Poetry*. New York: Dover Publications, 2005.

Peck, Henry T. *The New Baedeker 1856–1914, Being Casual Notes of an Irresponsible Traveler*. New York: Dodd, Mead, 1910.

Pia, Pascal. *Apollinaire par Lui-Même*. Paris: Éditions du Seuil, 1954.

Picasso, Pablo. *Picasso on Art*, comp. Dore Ashton. New York: Viking Press, 1972.

Pulitzer, Henry. *Where Is the* Mona Lisa? London: Pulitzer Press, 1967.

Reit, Seymour V. *The Day They Stole the* Mona Lisa. New York: Summit Books, 1981.

Richardson, John. *A Life of Picasso: The Prodigy, 1881–1906*. Vol. 1. New York: Random House, 1991.

————. *A Life of Picasso: The Cubist Rebel, 1907–1916.* Vol. 2. New York: Alfred A. Knopf, 1996.

————. *A Life of Picasso: The Triumphant Years, 1916–1932.* Vol. 3. New York: Alfred A. Knopf, 2008.

Rhodes, Henry. *Alphonse Bertillon.* London: Harrap, 1956.

Robertson, Charles. *International Herald Tribune.* New York: Columbia University Press, 1987.

Rubin, William, Seckel, Hélène, Cousins, Judith. *Les Demoiselles d'Avignon.* New York: Museum of Modern Art, distributed by Harry N. Abrams, Inc., 1994.

Saarinen, Aline B. *The Proud Possessors.* New York: Random House, 1958.

Sassoon, Donald. *Leonardo and the* Mona Lisa *Story: The History of a Painting Told in Pictures.* New York: Overlook Press, 2006.

————. *Becoming* Mona Lisa: *The Making of a Global Icon.* New York: Harcourt, 2001.

Schwartz, Lillian F. *The Computer Artist's Handbook.* New York: Norton, 1992.

Shattuck, Roger. *The Banquet Years.* New York: Anchor Books, 1958.

Simpson, Colin. *Artful Partners.* London: Bodley Head, 1987.

Spiel, Robert E. *Art Theft and Forgery Investigation.* Springfield, Ill.: Charles C. Thomas, 2000.

Steegmuller, Francis. *Guillaume Apollinaire, Poet Among the Painters.* New York: Farrar, Straus, 1963.

Stein, Gertrude. *The Autobiography of Alice B. Toklas.* New York: Knopf, 1990.

Stone, Melville E. *News-gathering.* New York: s.n., 1918.

Temperini, Renaud. *Leonardo da Vinci at the Louvre.* Paris: Réunion des Musées Nationaux, 2003.

Tomkins, Calvin. *Merchants and Masterpieces.* New York: Henry Holt, 1989.

Trumble, Angus. *Brief History of the Smile.* New York: Basic Books, 2003.

Turner, Richard. *Inventing Leonardo.* New York: Knopf, 1993.

Vasari, Giorgio. *The Lives of the Painters, Sculptors and Architects,* trans. Gaston du C. de Vere. London: Everyman Library, 1927.

Walker, John. *Self-Portrait with Donors.* Boston: Little, Brown, 1974.

Wright, Christopher. *The Art of the Forger.* New York: Dodd, Mead, 1985.

Meet with Interesting People
Enjoy Stimulating Conversation
Discover Wonderful Books

VINTAGE BOOKS / ANCHOR BOOKS

Reading Group Center
THE READING GROUP SOURCE FOR BOOK LOVERS

Visit ReadingGroupCenter.com where you'll find great
reading choices—award winners, bestsellers, beloved
classics, and many more—and extensive resources
for reading groups such as:

Author Chats
Exciting contests offer reading groups
the chance to win one-on-one phone
conversations with Vintage and Anchor
Books authors.

Extensive Discussion Guides
Guides for over 450 titles as well as
non–title specific discussion questions
by category for fiction, nonfiction,
memoir, poetry, and mystery.

Personal Advice and Ideas
Reading groups nationwide share ideas,
suggestions, helpful tips, and anecdotal
information. Participate in the discussion
and share your group's experiences.

Behind the Book Features
Specially designed pages which can include
photographs, videos, original essays, notes
from the author and editor, and book-related
information.

Reading Planner
Plan ahead by browsing upcoming
titles, finding author event schedules,
and more.

Special for Spanish-language reading groups
www.grupodelectura.com
A dedicated Spanish-language content
area complete with recommended titles
from Vintage Español.

A selection of some favorite reading group titles from our list

Atonement by Ian McEwan
Balzac and the Little Chinese Seamstress
  by Dai Sijie
The Blind Assassin by Margaret Atwood
The Devil in the White City by Erik Larson
Empire Falls by Richard Russo
The English Patient by Michael Ondaatje
A Heartbreaking Work of Staggering Genius
  by Dave Eggers
The House of Sand and Fog by Andre Dubus III
A Lesson Before Dying by Ernest J. Gaines

Lolita by Vladimir Nabokov
Memoirs of a Geïsha by Arthur Golden
Midnight in the Garden of Good and Evil
  by John Berendt
Midwives by Chris Bohjalian
Push by Sapphire
The Reader by Bernhard Schlink
Snow by Orhan Pamuk
An Unquiet Mind by Kay Redfield Jamison
Waiting by Ha Jin
A Year in Provence by Peter Mayle